I0617290

BUILDING DREAMS

FINDING PERSONAL AND FINANCIAL
FREEDOM THROUGH HEALING

BECKY HURLEY

HOUSE
PUBLISHING

HEARTS UNLEASHED HOUSE PUBLISHING

For information about special discounts for bulk purchases contact:
hearts@heartsunleashed.com

Manufactured in the United States of America
Library of Congress Cataloging-in-Publication Data Hurley, Becky.

Summary:
"Many people want success but find themselves at the intersection of confusion and burnout."
Building Dreams is the book that pulls back the curtain on why you haven't reached the levels of success you dream of. Written by your new bestie, Becky, this book is a guide through and beyond the obstacles that have kept you from building your most abundant life. This page turner will keep you interested in what happens to Becky and what will become possible for you.

Becky has forged her way through the fire of transformation and is dedicated to helping others free themselves from the chains of early life trauma and wounding. Many crave success but most are unwilling to walk the uncomfortable path of the healing journey. In this book, Becky makes the process understandable, relatable, and doable.

Setting your sights on success will surface all the trauma that you have successfully compartmentalized. We must heal the wounds we have previously, and unconsciously, tried to avoid or suppress. With a commitment to share your gifts, reach financial freedom, and enjoy a life of self acceptance and self expression, overcoming these obstacles is completely possible and this book will show you how.

This book will:

- Create awareness about the subconscious blocks between you and your success
- Move you through grief, shame, fear, and limitations
- Help you shed disempowering beliefs and programming
- Reveal how your past creates your present
- Offer you the opportunity to recognize and break the patterns of generational trauma
- Stop and prevent burnout
- Shine a light down the path of success and financial freedom
- Teach you the magic of money management
- Open your eyes to a whole new world of possibilities
- And so much more

ISBN: 979-8-9882783-5-1 (Paperback)
ISBN: 979-8-9882783-4-4 (Hardcover)

[1. Nonfiction. 2. Memoir. 3. Healing. 4. Self-Help. 5. Business. 6. Motivational]

DEDICATION

This book is dedicated to the dreamers, the doers, and the ones labeled rebels and troublemakers; the ones who see things differently. It is for the ones who feel like round pegs in square holes, trying to fit in. This is a place where you belong. This book is dedicated to you—the trailblazers.

TABLE OF CONTENTS

Preface

I was sitting on a grassy hillside, watching a dream fall apart before my very eyes. It was July 2015 in Wisconsin. Overlooking a beautiful valley of grass and trees, it was warm and sunny, but there seemed to be a rain cloud over my head. I was sitting on the land we had been planning to put a road and nine luxury homes in a custom-home subdivision.

Tears streamed down my face as I stared over the beautiful valley; the exact view that I imagined our homeowners would enjoy from their porches and patios. Instead of tears of joy, hope, and anticipation, I was coming to terms with the inevitable failure my husband and I were facing with this hopeless project. We had six of the nine lots pre-sold on a dream. The subdivision was in its development phase and that land was only a fraction of the hundred and twenty acres that we would be permanently turning into protected agricultural land. It was an extraordinary vision.

However, that dream was falling apart. It was turning into a huge failure. We chased a vision without the due diligence on our part. In our minds, we could see the subdivision completed but we had one major roadblock; the road. We needed a loan to put in a road which turned out to be a $350,000 project. Numerous banks turned us away and wouldn't lend us the money to put in the road, and we couldn't sell the lots if there was no access to them.

Eighteen months down the drain. Eighteen months of commitment. Eighteen months of attending meetings with the town board, planning commission, engineers, attorneys, and a realtor that became our land development mentor. Eighteen. Months. All for nothing.

What was I thinking? I was just a small town farm girl who

thought she could develop a subdivision. I felt so defeated, like I bit off more than I could chew. Maybe I had gotten ahead of myself or got too comfortable with risk taking.

We had gotten started in real estate five years prior and had been making our money on fix and flip homes. We were climbing year after year and became confident enough to try a subdivision. My husband, Noah, also had a banner year in his landscaping business. That year leading up to the project, we both earned more money than either of us had ever made in our lives.

We were feeling pretty on top of our world. We were ready to take chances and place bigger bets on our abilities, but I guess you could say we got a little too excited about the potential of this subdivision. We didn't think it all the way through, and we paid a hefty price. We had to pay another hefty price around the same time when we got hit with our income tax bill for making the most money we've ever made. That year got heavier and heavier by the minute.

As I sat on that hillside, all that weight was sitting right on top of my shoulders. I was embarrassed and my inner critic taunted me about getting 'too big for my britches' by playing a game I 'wasn't ready for.' I felt naive and immature but no matter how I felt, I was going to have to face the hard truth. This project was a bust.

Within a few months, the entire plan fell through and all we were left with was a $150,000 debt to pay back. Well, debt wasn't the only thing we were left with. My husband and I also acquired some serious headaches and anxiety over such a huge mistake. We had bills piled up and were faced with figuring out how to pay up with money we didn't have.

I had just quit my slightly-higher-than-minimum-wage job a year and a half earlier to leap into the unknown. I jumped into the world of entrepreneurship with a dream in my heart and a fire in my belly. I swiftly got my ass kicked and sent home like a dog with its tail between its legs. The door hit me in the ass on my way out, flung a $150,000 bill with it, and there I was crying on that hillside, wishing I could take it all back.

During this phase in my life, I very quickly fell into the most deeply depressed state I had ever known. I often refer to that time as *my year of depression.* Crying became part of my daily ritual. My mind raced in every direction, but I had very little clarity or motivation. It brought me to such a dark place that I encountered the devil at the depths of that year. I reached my lowest lows just after we had reached some of our highest highs.

I will share my struggles in much more detail as we get to know each other throughout this book, but right now I want to share what I realized as I was going through the pain of that year. If I can meet and know the devil, then inherently, I can meet and know God. This phase of life drew me closer to God, who pulled me up out of the darkness.

At the depths of my pain, I decided to start speaking to God. I admitted to him that I didn't know what to do and asked him for his help and guidance. "I'm ready for your help," I prayed. "Please guide me. Please help me!"

That was when things started to change from within. There was nothing immediately different outside of myself. We still had the debt. We were still struggling, but I could feel the shift of faith take over my life. It certainly wasn't fast, but gradually, everything started getting better.

Feeling inspired again, I started doing more things to change the trajectory of my life. I got serious about the inner work. I took on therapy, healing, setting boundaries, fitness, well-being, and more. With my faith intact and developing, I relied on the strength of God to help me get out of bed every morning and do the next right thing to come back from getting knocked down so hard.

As you join me for a journey through the trials and tribulations of my life, I hope to positively impact yours. I knew that I wanted to write a book when I started to realize that what I had learned could help others make their way through the challenges I had previously clawed my way out of. I hope to spare you a few bumps and bruises along the way, but I also know we all have our own journey.

You will learn a little bit about how hardheaded I can be when I set my sights on a goal, i.e. that whole subdivision saga, but being hardheaded is what I attribute my resilience to. It's what I credit our now multiplied success far beyond that $150,000 loss.

I know that as you walk your own path, you will have your own unique set of challenges. They are yours for good reason. They will show you what you are made of. They will shape you exactly the way they should to turn you into the leader that you are. From one leader to another, I am here to share my story and shed some light on some of the things that you don't know until you know. We will consciously talk about behaviors and identities that unconsciously run our lives. This is an opportunity for you to take your power back and take control over the quality and direction of your life.

I will share more about my upbringing and how the dysfunction I grew up in shaped me into a problem-solving, crime-fighting, house-building, empire-running badass. I will address how the trauma and toxicity of your past doesn't have to leak into your present and future. I will share the incredible magic of mindfulness practices. I will sprinkle in some cool money mindset work for you too, it's one of my favorite topics. Lastly but not leastly, I will offer you faith and if you feel like you don't have any right now, you can borrow mine. There's plenty where that comes from.

This book has been years, decades, in the making and I am thrilled to be with you right here, right now. If you have found your way to these words, welcome. It is no mistake. It is no coincidence. I trust that we are a perfect duo and this is the perfect book for where you are in your life and where you see yourself going.

When I began my healing journey, I leaned into getting support and it made all the difference in my life. I invite you to let yourself be supported by the lessons in these pages. Maybe that also means to start researching a therapist or coach. Maybe it is time for courses on financial freedom. Whatever you think you might need, consider that you know it is time to get more serious about what's possible for you.

As we wrap up this introduction and kick off this book, I want to offer the incredible possibility that you can have it all. There is abundance available to each of us if we are willing to receive it. Not only will I teach you that it is out there for the taking, I will show you how to manifest it in this lifetime. If this Midwestern farm girl can become a multi-millionaire mogul, you, my friend, can become whatever your beautiful heart desires. Let's do this.

Part 1

Chapter 1

Midwestern Mindset

"You choose and create a better life simply because you stand your ground and decide, "I'm worth this. I'm going to go after the life that I desire. I'm going to go after the life I've always dreamed of.""

For better or for worse, we are a product of our environment. We initially take on the beliefs of our parents and others who influenced us in our formative years. Even if we are not inherently like them, we tend to speak, walk, talk, and act like the people we grew up with because it is what we were exposed to. We often don't know any better until we start learning for ourselves, usually when we get a little older.

So much of our knowledge is based on our life experiences. You might notice how people often end up exactly or nothing like their family, but in either case, our upbringing shapes how we turn out. So many of the conclusions we draw about ourselves, others, and life are simply based on what we observe in our childhood; the time our brain is developing. Some people break the mold, but for the majority, 'the apple doesn't fall far from the tree.'

Being from the Midwest, so many of us were the same. It was natural to sort of 'fall in line' with everyone else, but that didn't mean that I fit in. I am a small town girl writing to you about being a multimillionaire mom, wife, and entrepreneur. There came a point in my life when I had to break the mold. I will expand more on that later, because I spent the first half of my life trying to live up to what I thought was expected of me in order to earn what I thought was due to me.

I grew up in a small farming community in Southwest Wisconsin. I grew up raising beef cattle and crops on a 500-acre farm that had been in our family dating back to the 1800's. We did not dairy farm like the traditional Wisconsin farmers. We had beef cows and horses. We used horses to round up the cattle, grew huge gardens every year, and ate mostly food grown on our own property.

I am from an area of the Midwest where no one goes over fifty-five mph, no one is in a hurry, and nothing changes too quickly. You can always see the stars at night and take the time to appreciate them as well. It is a slow-paced, tight-knit community of farm families. Especially at the time I was growing up, the parents worked together and the kids worked on the farm as well.

A good part of our family's income came from the farm so we all had our fair share of work to contribute. I'm the youngest of four siblings and we would all work together on the chores. It was our family bonding time. We would bale hay in the summers and haul wood in the winters. In the Midwest, especially on the farm, we were raised with a strong work ethic and taught to take pride in our efforts.

I always felt like I was living such an awesome life. My dearest grade school friends and I would ride horses back and forth down the road. I was really involved in 4H, FFA, and raising animals. We had lots of barn kitties and farm animals to play with and lived a typical country life you might imagine. I loved that way of life. I got to grow up doing work I loved in a community I enjoyed. Even as a grown woman who has seen more of the world, I still prefer country living.

My upbringing was this all-American farm family picture, on the outside. Looking in, it was very different. As you dive deeper into these pages, and into my life, I am going to fill you in on what happened behind closed doors. I am going to share the darker side of the Midwest Mindset that shaped some of my best and worst traits and the trauma it caused me. I will share about the physical and emotional scars of growing up in an abusive household and a lot about why freedom is so important to me.

Yes, this book was originally meant to be all about financial freedom but on a deeper level, this is a traumatized child's guide to healing from a world of hurt. This is a manual to use in creating your independence, realizing your capability, owning your value, prioritizing your mental health, and generating emotional freedom. We are going to take a beautiful journey together. We may have not gone without the necessities but what was missing in our home was love, connection, and communication. This story is not rags to riches. It's a tale of knock-down drag-outs to multi-million-dollar cash outs. It's a guide to help you realize that your 'struggle' is unique to you and that no matter what challenges you've been through, you can have any future you can dream up.

I will take you through a lot of *my* life, but I put this book together with you in mind. In fact, this book was a bunch of tear-stained journal entries to process so much of what has happened to me. I wrote this book for me, I published it for you. I *know* the power of healing and I want to do everything in my power to offer that kind of liberation to you. I am excited and honored that we are at this point together.

Something that is important for me to say as we begin is that by many accounts, I don't have a rags to riches story in terms of not having enough money, growing up poor, or wondering where my next meal would come from. It feels important to me to preface this book by saying this because in my story, we had enough. My parents were both college educated. They worked hard. They both had jobs. My mom was a registered nurse, my dad was a teacher, and together they farmed five hundred acres. We did not go 'without' in terms of having our physical needs met. We had food, water, clothing, and shelter.

I have known for about ten years that I would write a book such as this and I stopped myself many times because I discredited my 'struggle.' I judged myself harshly, thinking "so many people had it so much worse. Who do you think you are? Why are you so special? You don't even know real struggle."

I talked myself out of starting more times than I am willing to admit. After beginning my healing journey and sharing my story in therapy and coaching, hearing myself talk about my life helped me realize, *"wow, I did go through some wild shit!"* and I finally felt ready to share.

I have dedicated my life to helping people realize that you can go through hard times and come out the other side. You can go through abusive situations and go on to create multimillion dollar companies, healthy marriages, and a happy family. You can do that. You choose it. You choose and create a better life simply because you stand your ground and decide, "I'm worth this. I'm going to go after the life that I desire. I'm going to go after the life I've always dreamed of."

For the rest of this book, I am going to show you exactly how I did that and how you can do it too. Let's get started.

Chapter 2

The 911 Call
That Never Happened

"I grew up feeling like we had to tiptoe around the house, always walking on eggshells, because a massive blowup could happen at any time."

"Dad, stop it! Dad, knock it off!" I screamed as I watched him pushing and chasing my sister down the stairs, out of the house, and down the hill until she ran into her boyfriend's car to escape. My screams were muffled, lost in the chaos of fury that was happening.

I was ten years old and my sister was home from college for the weekend. My mother would never say she had a favorite but out of the four of us kids, I have always believed that she loved my sister the most. Every time she came home, my mom and I would clean the house from top to bottom; vacuuming, dusting, sweeping, mopping, cleaning the bathrooms, and getting it ready for her arrival. It was always a special event when she would make her way home.

We were having an otherwise normal weekend on the farm, horseback riding and hanging out until she had to get ready to head back to college. On her way out, my mom offered her some cans of soup to take back to college. My dad saw the cans of soup in her hands and burst into a fit of rage. He assumed she was stealing them.

My memory is kind of a whirlwind from there. My dad always

seemed to bring a storm of rage into the house. It didn't matter what set him off, it was always going to cause damage and watching him push and shove my sister around made me want to save her from the damage he was currently causing.

I had recently learned in school about calling 911 in emergencies. I remember standing by the desk in our house, where the phone sat, picking up the receiver with my trembling hand hovering over the numbers.

"What are you doing?" My mom scolded when she saw me holding the phone with my thumb hovering over the 9.

"I'm calling 911!" I responded frantically, short of breath.

"We don't do that here," she said in a stern, solemn tone.

My throat got tight. A wave of hopelessness whooshed down my neck and shoulders. Immediately, the phone felt like a hundred pounds. I looked at it longingly, wishing those three numbers would dial themselves and someone would come save us. Instead, I numbly hung up the phone and continued watching my dad's eruption.

I watched my sister crying and running to her boyfriend's car. I watched her leave the driveway, with tears in my eyes and a lump in my throat, wishing I could drive away with her.

I wanted to call 911 because I wanted my dad to learn a lesson. I wanted there to be a consequence to his actions. I wanted him to stop acting crazy. I wanted him to stop behaving that way.

Deeper than that, I wanted him to not be angry anymore. He was always so angry, but I hung up the phone like my mom told me to because I knew that if I called 911, they would take my dad away. I definitely hated how we were living behind closed doors, but I didn't want them to take him away. I just wanted the torment to stop.

I wanted to have the family that everyone thought we had. I will not say that I didn't have a good childhood, on the outside, I did. In the eyes of the general public, we were an upstanding family in the community. We were a family of teachers, nurses, 4-H members, track athletes, band members, and farmers. I truly loved growing up raising horses and living in the country. I loved the farming lifestyle.

The part that nobody got to see was that the tension in our household was fueled by my dad's fear, anger, and aggression. There was a lot of this "unsettledness" in our household and as a result, I grew up feeling 'on edge' a lot of the time. I grew up feeling like we had to tiptoe around the house, always walking on eggshells, because a massive blowup could happen at any time.

Physical, verbal, mental, and emotional abuse were the norm every day. Eruptions went on daily, nightly, always. It was like living in a house where the floors were made of hot coals that you only ran over if you really needed to get a snack from the fridge and then duck back into your room or run outside to go work on the farm with the animals or crops.

When I think of my childhood, I think of the fighting. As I share this with you, I feel a heat in my cheeks about the physical and verbal abuse we endured for decades. I just so desperately wanted to be the people on the inside that the rest of our community saw us as on the outside, but that never happened, the same way I never called 911 that day.

Chapter 3

Behind Closed Doors

*"Whether your trauma is in your past or present,
it can be left behind in a way that doesn't keep you held back
from going for everything you pray for and envision."*

Tensions between my parents ran high. Their marriage was rocky to say the very least. Even at a very young age, I knew their marriage wasn't healthy, but I didn't want them to get divorced because I assumed that would mean I wouldn't get to live on the farm. I didn't want to leave the farm because I loved living there. I loved living in the country. I loved everything about our life, and so did my mom and my sister and brothers. We loved everything except the fighting; the heartache; the tension; the horror; the terror; the scariness. I think we all tolerated my parents' relationship for so long because of what we were afraid to lose.

We still went on family trips, enjoyed horseback rides together, and fared well in daily life but that was all part of the problem. We had this stark contrast between what was great and what was unspeakably terrible. Life was an internal and external battle at all times.

I will teach more about domestic violence as we go on but I want to say at this moment that this kind of abuse goes on for generations because it's 'not that bad.' The good seems to help us reason with the bad as if physical, verbal, and emotional abuse are okay as long as your parents stay together, you have horses, and can sign up for whatever extracurriculars you want. This justification looks different in different families and relationships, but we all have our reasons to tolerate the hard times. This made the abuse more difficult to understand because 'how could it be so good and so bad?'

There is a term called 'gaslighting' where an abuser manipulates their target and successfully reverses the situation to make it the victim's fault. This is confusing and demoralizing. For a victim of abuse who also believes it is their fault, breaking the cycle can be incredibly difficult. I've seen this happen my whole life. I experienced it first-hand in my family, but I mostly saw it in my mom.

I prayed and wished so much that my parents would learn to get along. I had spent at least twenty-four years of my life as their unofficial marriage counselor, literally sitting between the two of them and making them talk about their feelings. I even got into physical fights with my dad to fend him off my mom. I would constantly try to play mediator for them. I felt like I was on playground patrol in elementary school where we learned how to get kids to sit down, make amends with each other, and play nice.

They were a team in many ways, but they did not have any communication skills. My mom cared for the household and my dad cared for the farm. Their marriage was more of an entrapment to turn us four kids into civil, upstanding humans, get us college educations, and send us out the door all while keeping the five-hundred-acre farm going with two off-the farm jobs. The responsibilities outweighed anyone's needs or wellbeing. They communicated in the form of screaming at one another. Bickering and arguments regularly erupted into physical brawls and emotional screams for help. I will never forget the first night I started getting involved in their fights.

Growing up, I shared a room with my sister. We had a circular opening in the floor between our beds where a chimney pipe used to come up, back when there was a wood stove in the living room. It was now covered with a decorative black cast iron grate, but it was still open to the living room below. There were many times that you could vividly hear the arguments happening right underneath us. They always took place in the kitchen/dining room area.

One night, I woke up and blinked my eyes a few times. I heard something through the cast iron grate, and I started to feel nervous. I knew something was wrong. I held my breath and leaned up in my bed to listen. I sat very still. I heard the shuffling of feet which made my heart race and I gasped for air when I heard a shriek of terror, "Oh, God!"

It was my mom's voice, and I was jolted into action. I jumped out of my bed, ran out of our room, and listened intently down the stairwell of our old farmhouse. My dad was angry. He sounded so vicious. I could practically feel his teeth clenched together as he was spewing something terrifying about what he was going to do to my mother.

Panicked, I quickly woke up my sister. Our brothers shared a room across the hall, so I woke them all up and asked them to listen. I asked them if they could hear what was happening downstairs. They did. They heard it too and were listening.

"Why don't you do something?!" I pleaded with them. I was just five and they were twelve, fourteen, and seventeen years old. They stayed in their rooms, shook their heads, and told me not to go down there. I was shocked and upset. How could they not stop this? Someone, *anyone,* needed to do something and in that moment, I decided it would be me.

I took it upon myself to mobilize into action. If no one else was going to do anything to help or to put a stop to what was happening, I would do it myself. I was afraid and scared but I went for it anyway.

I ran as quickly as I could down the steep, narrow steps, trying not to trip and roll all the way down, which wasn't uncommon. I ran around to the kitchen area where my parents were in the middle of a heated fight. I joined a scene that would become all too familiar in time; my dad's ferocious, werewolf-like temper and my mom hunched over, quivering, whimpering, and crying. It wouldn't be the first time I would run down to see my dad with a death grip on my mother's arms and while she was shaking helplessly.

Without thinking, I ran right into the middle of them. I ran right toward the fire, like a warrior in Braveheart getting ready to ride my horse into battle and screamed at the top of my lungs for them to stop fighting. I was scared for my parents. I was also scared for myself, but I did it anyway because I felt it was what I had to do at the time. Because I wedged myself between them, they split up, but that didn't stop them from glaring at each other or spewing hateful things across the room at each other.

This happened daily for years. Little did I know this would continue until I was twenty-three years old. It was an interesting cycle of abuse. Tension ran rampant in our house. In fact, none of us called it 'abuse' until we were adults but that's exactly what it was. We just called it arguing, fighting, and tension, never abuse or domestic violence. Those were big, scary words. I didn't even know those terms until much later in life; much later than I was exposed to it.

To this day, I know this is where my inner warrior came from. I've always been ready for battle. I have reflexes like a mountain lion, ready to pounce on the bad guy at any time. This has served me well in many areas of life but ultimately it is a trauma response that I have had to become responsible for. I unknowingly adopted the rescuer role of what I now know as the 'trauma triangle;' abuser, victim, and rescuer. Blowups would happen nearly every night. They were comparable to the scariest horror movie scenes you've ever watched. Seething teeth, blood-curdling screams, and objects or body parts getting slammed into the walls.

What felt so painful about this was how we just kept getting up the next day and pretending like nothing happened the night before. Mom just had some new bruises on her arms, and we were supposed to act like it was no big deal or anything. That was what everyday life was like for us growing up.

"Why don't you get a divorce?" I once asked my mom after another morning of new bruises. I had just learned about that word in my elementary school class, probably from another classmate whose parents were splitting up.

"That's not what we do," she replied matter-of-factly.

Something's not right, I remember thinking. *Living with bruises, which are usually caused by pain, is not how my dad should treat my mom. No one should have bruises on them from someone else and continue to be involved with that person.* I hated the way she put up with all the violence and harm. At the time, I also didn't realize the role she played in it all.

I wanted both of my parents to be happy. To be normal. I just wanted them to love each other, be kind to each other, and laugh with each other. I don't think I ever heard them laugh together. Deep down, I loved my dad but hated the way his rage and my mom's need to live in misery added fuel to the fire that destroyed our family.

After countless disappointments over the years, I eventually learned that I can't save people. Even to this day, I have to actively remind myself to keep my Rescuer in check. I have to remember that people have to save themselves. *Only* they can save themselves and if they don't, that means they are not ready to. In my youth, I could only hope that the grace of God would save us.

However, I began questioning our faith and the values of the church. We maintained our status in the community that we were an upstanding, homegrown, farm family with faith in God because we were members of the local church. It felt like such a lie because nobody mentioned that on our way home from church we would nearly have car wrecks due to my mom and dad arguing in the front seat. I usually held my breath on the drive back, praying for God's saving grace.

In regards to faith, I was lucky to have a childhood best friend who had an intense faith in God. She taught me more about prayers, the Bible, and God than I had learned anywhere else. She was one of the only ones that knew what happened behind closed doors in those early years.

Once my parents got more comfortable with any of my friends, they would let their guard down and show some of their true selves. Some arguments would erupt while I was on the phone with friends or even when I had someone over for a sleepover. It was embarrassing to say the least.

It may sound sort of messed up but I was so grateful she overheard things on the phone and experienced the fighting. It was refreshing to know I had a friend who knew about my home life so I didn't have to pretend with her. She knew that fights happened on the regular and oddly, I found comfort in her knowing. I could be open with her and because of that, I felt open to what she taught me about God.

She helped me keep my faith in God when there was no evidence of his presence in my home. I remember her and her mom teaching me about being born again and accepting Jesus as my savior. I prayed and read my Bible regularly. As a result of that, I believed God lived inside me and that he was always with me. This brought so much peace to my tumultuous life. I am so thankful to God, for the Angels, and the people along the way who have helped me get through such a traumatic upbringing. My faith kept me sane in a lot of insane circumstances. My faith is what helped me get through those years of surviving a situation I had no way out of. It was what I held onto when I had nowhere else to turn and I was living in survival mode.

When I first dreamt up this book, I had a very different vision for it but when I started to write it, I knew my story had to be told. I really didn't want to include this part of my story in my book. I wanted to skip straight to the how to have a successful life, marriage, and business part. I had hoped to bypass the details of my upbringing because well, I assumed my parents would eventually read this and also, I really wish this wasn't my story.

However, this was my story. It took me a long time to accept that I couldn't sugarcoat my experience enough to sound motivational. It can be downright upsetting at times. However, I decided to include a more honest version of my childhood because it shaped so much of who I am and it's gotten me where I am today. Like I mentioned in chapter one, we either fall right by the family tree or we stray off as far as we possibly can from it. I ran as far as I could and as quickly as I could, but it didn't change anything about how I grew up.

Even God can't change the past, so I am not going to tell you how I became a millionaire without telling you some of the most integral parts of my story. Sharing this part of my past scares the shit out of me because it is not my mission for you to walk away from this book thinking about what an asshole my dad is or why mom put up with it. It is not about saying 'poor Becky' or judging my life. It is about normalizing how to accept how our whole lives have gone, not just the cute parts. I am especially not telling my history to compare trauma as better or worse. Trauma is not a competition.

I am sharing fully and boldly because I am a living, breathing testament that you can overcome your past and have a tremendous future beyond your wildest dreams. I'm owning up to it all because if it can help anyone realize you too are done being treated poorly, maybe this will inspire you to own your past, heal it, release it, and make a better life for yourself.

Whether your trauma is in your past or present, it can be left behind in a way that doesn't keep you held back from going for everything you pray for and envision. I am going to teach you how to create freedom of all sorts. Financial freedom happens to be one of my personal favorites to teach but we can't get there if we don't break free of the mental imprisonment of our shame and pain.

Chapter 4

Wishing For More

"I wished for more my entire life and I knew as a grown woman that I would be the one to provide myself a better life."

At eight years old, I was sitting on the hillside below my house at the end of a long day. I took in the whole view, looking out on the valley, toward all the hills and trees. I took a good long look at our beautiful old red barn where generations of family have farmed. I could sense the decades of legacy on my shoulders and felt pride in my chest. I loved living there. I loved the history of knowing my ancestors had lived there, raising animals and babies. Even as a young girl, I always felt so connected to my heritage and planned to carry on tradition.

It was late afternoon, and I knew the sun would soon be sinking below the tall hills of the valley behind me. As I took one last glance around, I spotted a dandelion puff next to my foot. I had just recently learned about making wishes on the floating wisps of these magical little blessings. I looked at the dandelion puff and swirled it around in my fingers.

I thought hard about the wish I wanted to make. I didn't want to ask for just any wish. I didn't want something materialistic, like a barbie or a toy. Wishing for small things wasn't for me. That wasn't how my brain worked. Besides, I had most of the *things* I wanted and needed so I didn't want to waste it. I wanted something more meaningful and then, I made up my mind. I picked it up, took a deep breath, and thought of my wish as I blew its wisps into the wind.

"I wish for a good life," I thought longingly.

I felt short of breath as I blew wishfully. It felt like a tall order that my family could be normal. For as long as I can remember, I just wanted to have a good life; a safe home. I wanted to be happy. I wanted there to be love in our home and feel that love in my heart.

Wanting a good life became the wish that I would hope for from then on out. I made it with every birthday candle I'd blow out and every dandelion puff I swirled around in my fingers.

As a young girl, I realized the kind of marriage *I* wanted because of what was missing from my parents' marriage. I knew from a young age that wasn't how relationships were supposed to be. I knew we didn't live like most families. I decided very early on that I wanted nothing like what my parents had, and I set my heart on a better life with every wish. I wanted to love and be loved by my life partner. Nothing else would do. It became something I looked forward to and dreamt about for years.

I may have had these dreams of a better life but what I was seeing on a day-to-day basis was very different. Whenever my dad watched television, if the Packers weren't playing, my dad would watch old Westerns. The good guys vs. bad guys movies with John Wayne and Clint Eastwood shooting off guns, having bar fights, and slapping women.

I used to sit and watch them with him and once in a while, I would see a man hit a woman across the face. It made me wince and my stomach would churn. Even to this day, that sound rings in my ears and makes the hair on the back of my neck stand up.

My dad grew up in an era where it wasn't considered out-of-line to slap your wife. It wasn't considered out of the ordinary to use an aggressive scare tactic with your wife; to clench your teeth and use seething words against her. It was considered normal. It was normal to keep your wife 'in check.' It was normal to be the authoritative man of the house. It may have even been encouraged to keep your reign, rule, and order in the home, especially with your strength and intimidation tactics.

I can assume that now because he never apologized for anything. He never acted like he was doing anything wrong. I would constantly insist that he apologize to my mom, but he always justified his behavior.

"Didn't you hear the way she was talking to me?! She deserved it! She's a liar!" he would shout at me.

He would go on blaming, she would go on whimpering, and I would go on mediating. Being the youngest, it took me much longer to catch on than my older siblings. They coped and dealt with it in their own ways. Heck, maybe they had tried before I was born but by the time I came around, I was fighting battles I didn't belong in and they had already checked out.

I hated the angry outbursts. There were too many nights of arguments and fighting and hatred and anger to count. I hated living in fear, just wondering when the next blowup would happen. It was like walking on glass. Every step felt dangerous, and I am *still* healing from that level of danger. Often, I catch myself being tense for no reason because I grew up 'braced for impact.' I have to make a conscious effort to relax and remember that I am safe now, but years of that lifestyle has its effects.

What always made it worse was the pretending. Whether it be in public or at home, we were all expected to just act like nothing traumatic happened the night before. It would be the next morning and my dad would be in the kitchen acting like nothing was wrong. He would be frying up food and asking us how we wanted our eggs. Like it was no big deal. Well, it *was* a big deal.

I hated giving in to his behavior. It made me hate him. My dad would never apologize, and he never faced a consequence. Instead, we would just pick up the pieces and keep going about our lives. This cycle went on for years and years. Eventually, I got away from it when I moved away for college and then out on my own. For years, I would stop talking to my parents for a few months at a time but I would always go back and eventually, I would always 'break the ice' again.

For a while, I would go back for the desire of a normal, cohesive family but that was never the case. It was one traumatizing experience after another. One shitty memory after another, all which I had to hide. One time, I didn't hide it very well when I was on the phone with a college boyfriend, who was on his way to my house to visit.

He lived an hour away and we were on the phone when I heard my parents start fighting. I jolted into action and was so upset I started punching and shoving my dad back yelling, "Stop hitting my mom! Stop hitting my mom!" I fought him off and when I finally caught my breath, I lost it again immediately.

I was horrified to realize that I hadn't hung up the phone and my boyfriend was on the other end, listening to the eruption. I cringed as I picked the phone back up to see if he had actually just heard all of that, and he sure did.

"I am pulled over on the side of the road, is everyone okay over there?!?" he asked, completely taken aback.

"Yeah, tonight's not a good night. You should just head home," I said, so embarrassed. I hung up and gave up. I hated this life we were living. I was excited to escape to college, but this chaos continued after we had all flown the coop.

It continued until my mom left my dad for good when I was twenty-three years old. He had finally hurt her for the last time. They were in another fight about who knows what when she ended up with two cracked ribs from Dad pushing her into the couch and she fell over the coffee table. It was about two weeks before Thanksgiving and all of us children were already out on our own.

We hadn't known where she was for two weeks, and we were all so concerned. She was supposed to come visit me in Lake Geneva, where I was living for my first year of teaching. We were supposed to have a girl's weekend together except, when I was done with school that Friday, I had two voicemails on my phone.

"Hi Becky, I'm in a safe place," she said in a voicemail from a phone number I didn't recognize. "I'm not within reach of a phone, so you can't really get a hold of me."

The next message was from my dad explaining that he came home from a meeting and my mom was gone and he didn't know where she was. Those two messages weren't the ideal way to end my day. I felt right back in the middle of my parents' relationship, and it was the exact reason I had finally left.

By Thanksgiving we still didn't know where my mom was because she couldn't share. We knew it was for her safety but not knowing was nerve wracking. We didn't know if she was with a friend, a relative, a hospital, or a hideaway cabin somewhere. It was a mystery.

In the meantime, since our matriarch was gone, I took on the role of getting food together for the cold, quiet, heartless, sad Thanksgiving meal our family had. It was, and still is, an excruciating memory. I went to a local deli to get take-out turkey, gravy, mashed potatoes, and salads for our family to have for our Thanksgiving dinner. Not knowing where our mom was, we ate in silence.

My dad just shook his head in disgust and blame. After my mom left, for years my dad would say things like, "She's greedy. She left because she's greedy." Our dad never learned his lesson. He just learned how to justify his own victimhood. He convinced himself that she was greedy because now he had to learn how to do his own taxes, learn to cook for himself, and do his own laundry for the first time in his life. He had to learn to take care of himself because now, no one was going to do it for him or put up with his temper. It was minor in comparison to his offenses, but I felt some justice was served.

At first, I was scared of my mom's disappearance because we didn't know where she was. There were many times when my parents fought that my mom would just take off in her car and leave. It was very scary as a child. I always assumed she just went for a drive to cool off to get away, but it was fine because she always came back. Finally, she didn't come back. Prior to my mom leaving, I had nightmares of her taking things into her own hands and ending her life. I was always scared for her, so knowing that she was safe and getting help gave me a huge sense of relief.

She finally came out of hiding after about two weeks away. She let us know that she had spent that time in a women's shelter thirty minutes from our home. I didn't even know that existed. I guessed she had been researching a safe place to go in case she ever did need to run away and leave.

The only way she agreed to come out of the women's shelter was to meet my dad in court to file a four-year-long restraining order against him. The four of us siblings understood exactly why my mom did that. To the rest of our neighbors, family members, and friends, this was a shock. No one knew what happened behind our closed doors.

My mom had the restraining order installed on my dad for her own protection and she came to my house in Walworth to stay until she could find something. I remember the sad look on her face as she pulled into the driveway of the house I was renting when she had finally moved off the farm. She had this car the size of a boat, a Ford Crown Victoria, stuffed to the roof with everything she could fit into it. She had our old green cooler in the trunk for food. My heart ached for her.

Eventually, she had asked if she could just live with me but at twenty-three years old, in my first real job out of college, I was at my capacity trying to figure out enough on my own. I wasn't ready or willing to have my mom live with me. Later, in therapy, I learned that constantly asking me to rescue her was something a parent should not impose on a child. I also learned that even when I did try to make things better for her she would always create more misery in her life. She found comfort in misery. I later learned that this was a trauma response she carried forward from her prior childhood trauma I knew nothing about.

I also knew that I didn't want to be the middleman in between my parents anymore. I had already spent far too much of my life trying and failing at that. I did my best to point out what was going on so they could correct it. I tried so hard. I spent seventeen years of my own life trying for them. In the end, nothing was going to change.

After all my years of trying to bring them together, trying to help them get along, I was relieved that it was over.

Additionally, I didn't have the know-how to muddle through their divorce matters and pick up the pieces for my mom. I knew it was going to be heavy and I didn't have the strength to carry her through that. To top it off, I was ready to live my own life. I was just getting my start when they were ending their marriage. I had just landed a great job. My future was bright, and I wanted it to stay headed in that forward direction.

For my entire childhood, I always blamed my dad for the way we lived but it was in my young adult years that I started to see my mom's role in it all. My mom got off with a hall pass because I viewed her as the victim, but she was just as much to blame. To sum it up, my parents suited each other. Abuser and victim, victim and abuser. They both felt like the victim of the other, but they abused differently. Looking back at the way it all played out, she was just as bad as my dad in her own ways. My dad may have been more overt and physical, but my mom had her own strategies as well. Because I was so young, seeing her get hit, bruised, and yelled at made me want to defend her. Even though she wasn't physically abusive, all of her true colors came out later down the road as I tried to help her. In my adult years, I saw the way she identifies with that victim role and plays it to her advantage.

This was a true struggle and disappointment for me and took me much longer to see, understand, and accept. It was only after I started doing my own healing work that I came to understand everyone's role in toxic relationships. As I started to understand different forms of abuse, my mom's patterns and behaviors in victimhood became glaringly obvious.

I always sort of pitied her in the way that I excused her from any responsibility. I thought she deserved the world for all the years of torment but in retrospect, she was an active participant in the relationship. I am certainly glad she got out of that situation, and I would never say that anyone ever deserves abuse. I have simply learned how people end up and stay in those situations. I have come to understand how the mind and heart can work in a way that would attract us to situations like that. I will teach much more about that throughout this book.

In so many ways, I viewed my mom as a warrior in her own right. My mom suffered immeasurable abuse and trauma during a thirty-six-year marriage. She nearly died with each pregnancy from preeclampsia. She was scoffed at for getting pregnant for a fourth time. Each pregnancy was so high risk. They told her she was crazy for having another baby. And yet, she went through with the pregnancy and had me. Every single day I am grateful to her and God for my life. Without her I wouldn't be here, but I could also no longer excuse her for her role in it all and the way her emotional manipulation continued beyond my parents' divorce.

When I would look at this as a grown woman, I noticed her gluttony for punishment. It is a part of her identity to suffer. I mean it with my whole heart that I would go to the ends of the earth for my mother and in many ways, I feel like I have. I feel like if there were an edge of the Earth, I would have fallen off by now for how far I have gone trying to help her live a better life, but I had to accept that you cannot want healing and peace for someone more than they want it for themselves.

This was a painful realization for me that forced me to reconsider my relationship and boundaries with her, but I did, and I know it is for the better for her, me, and my family. As mentioned, my parents were suited for each other in their own right. That doesn't make it healthy, and the end of their relationship was essential. However, allowing some distance in my relationships with them became essential too. I wished for more for my entire life and I knew as a grown woman that I would be the one to provide myself a better life.

Chapter 5

Going Out on a Limb

*"Standing in your truth is investing. It is investing in yourself.
It's betting on you. If you wouldn't bet on yourself,
you can bet no one else will want to either."*

The summer before my freshman year of college, I had an internship in the mountains of Montana. I got to live out my cowgirl dreams. I worked on a cattle ranch with three hundred fifty angus cattle and two hundred sheep. I got to build fences, ride horses, and herd cattle through the mountains. I was fulfilling a childhood dream and it certainly felt like a dream. It was like I had died and gone to Heaven.

This internship was actually for a family friend that we knew from our hometown in Wisconsin. They had bought this ranch and I was honored and excited to have such an amazing opportunity. I will share quite frequently throughout this book exactly *how much* I love the farming and ranching lifestyle. Even in my financial freedom, where I can choose any lifestyle for my family, I choose the country. It is in my blood and heart. This summer internship was a real-life peak time for me. I loved the experience, and I loved being away from home.

There were a *lot* of great things about my life growing up. I learned so much from my lifestyle and had a lot of good times but it's hard to think about the good times without thinking about the hard times... the really hard times. Even my time away from home was littered with abuse and manipulation.

I remember regularly receiving threatening 5:30am phone calls from home. I would hear from my dad, "if you don't get home by *this date* you might as well not count yourself a part of our family anymore!"

I was their youngest and the last to leave the nest. With me gone, my parents had no one but each other to focus on and no one to throw in the middle. I would imagine they had a shocking look into their lives as empty nesters which included realizing how terrible their relationship was. I am sure the threatening phone calls were pleas in disguise.

Beyond the logistics of the farm, I don't think my dad could stand the idea of me not being around to have control over "what goes on in his house." Even with me gone, I was still considered 'under his roof.' Therefore, the threats continued near and far. This remained true for the first three decades of my life, even after I was moved out and married: more on that later.

I was only in Montana for six weeks and I was questioned weekly about "Why are you staying out there?" "When are you coming home?" "You better get back here!"

Yes, those calls were threatening but something happened when I got away from home, even for six weeks. Time away from the trauma activated my hunger for freedom. I got a taste of the sweetness of living on my own, away from the chaos and turmoil. No matter how much they barked at me over the phone, I made the choice to stay, and I stood my ground. I was doing work I loved and I was having the time of my life. I wasn't going to let it end over a few nasty phone calls. Those were the kinds of threats that I got on a regular basis anyway. I knew the drama would be waiting for me when I got back, no matter when I got back.

Predictably, it was. At the end of my first year of college, my dad helped me buy a ten-year-old car. Its sole purpose was to drive home on the weekends to help on the farm. I drove home to work on the farm weekend after weekend. During my college internship that summer, I was working on the university farm where I helped take care of the pigs, drive tractors, haul crops, and bale hay. As soon as my dad found out that I didn't come home one weekend because I went to a friend's house instead, both of my parents drove to my college apartment building in the middle of the night to confiscate my car until further notice. There was a battle for control that seemed never ending.

This continued on for so many years in so many ways, until I decided to break away. I had other plans for my life. I had a different set of goals that didn't mesh well with my family's idea of life. This is when I decided to start breaking away from the cycles of abuse and trauma.

Later in my life, and later in this book, I will share how I stepped away from my family in a big way. For the purpose of this book, I want to first share how I decided to break away from the mentality that would have kept me mostly broke, proving myself, pleasing others, and hustling for the rest of my days.

There were four of us children and at different points, I am sure we all thought we would get the farm and at other points, none of us wanted it. It simply became a manipulation tactic that my dad would use, holding the farm 'over our heads' as a threat to control us or get what he wanted from us. The farm was this 'golden egg' we were all trying to win.

He would threaten us with some sentiment of, "if you don't do what I'm asking, then you'll lose your chance at inheriting the farm. So, you better do as I say."

My father knew he had an advantage on us. There is an unspoken understanding that you either inherit a farm or marry into one to make any money farming. Starting from scratch as a first-generation farmer does not always pan out financially. There are a lot of front-end investments that take generations to turn a profit on. This is a well-known fact within the farming community and my father took full advantage of that leverage he had on us. He was third generation, and I was very interested in being the fourth.

For years I played along with it, truly. It wasn't a game I knew I was playing. I totally thought I would inherit that farm and live happily ever after on it with Noah and my children. I figured we would carry on the family legacy, keep traditions alive, and hand it down generation after generation, but after years of my dad's baiting me with it, I woke up from the game we were playing.

I finally had the realization that the cycle of physical, verbal, mental, and emotional abuse was never going to end unless I ended it. And by ending it, I mean I had to leave. "I left my dad," if there is such a thing.

In our final argument, he told me that his mother would be embarrassed by the person I had become. At that point in my life, I was self-employed as an entrepreneur and business owner, building homes, and investing in real estate and still holding onto the dream of farming. I was hustling my ass off and doing the best I could to *be* the best I could. To this day, I'm not even sure what he meant by that, other than to hurt me, but it was the final straw for me.

I never got to meet my grandmother, but I have to believe that she would more likely be embarrassed of the way her son was treating his family. Beyond the fact that he just said that to hurt me, the fact that my grandmother was a 'farmland flipper' long before flipping properties was popular tells me that her fire, her will, and her determination is in me. Here I am flipping houses and dominating the real estate industry just like my grandma. I may have never met her, but I simply wouldn't let my manipulative dad use his mother against his own daughter. There never seemed to be a 'too low' for him to go.

I refused to play the sick games anymore. I left my dad that day in April of 2016. That argument would be the last time he could hurt me. I decided then and there that it was on me to strike out and blaze my own trail. I didn't have to be the fourth generation to farm that same land in order to carry on the tradition of farming in my family. I could get my start on any land that felt right to me and my family.

Once I changed my mindset, I realized I would prefer it be my own, finding it on my own, and making it my own.

The foundation of land I grew up on is built on old wounds, hurt, and abuse. I would need to burn down the house I grew up in to get rid of the haunting memories of bruises made, screams and cries for help, and the many tears that were shed behind closed doors. I no longer wanted that land or anything that would come with it. I was ready for a fresh start.

One of the harder parts about breaking away from domestic violence and manipulation was that nobody saw what we experienced. A common trait of these situations is that the abuser appears very friendly, charismatic, and even popular in day-to-day life. My dad was a teacher and so many viewed him with respect and admiration, but nobody saw the husband and father behind closed doors. It can be so confusing for people to comprehend because of the way it was hidden and discrete. The scars I have are mostly emotional, and therefore, hard for people to understand why I wanted to get away so badly.

Once I finally saw the way he was using that land to control our behaviors, I became immediately sick of it. Suddenly, I had hit a point of frustration and defeat and I no longer wanted it. I had a lot of grief about the loss of my life-long dream, especially after going to college for agriculture and being the only one of my four siblings working in an agriculture-related career. I had to accept that even if he planned to give me the farm, the cost was nowhere near worth the reward. At that point, the manipulation and guilt trips weren't working anymore. I mentally and emotionally surrendered my desire to inherit that land and knew I would have to make a life of my own.

People in my life, even those who said they supported me, changed their minds about that when I took a stand against being manipulated and mistreated. At that point, it didn't matter. They didn't see what was happening behind closed doors and they weren't willing to believe it. I was creating an obvious boundary between me and the things that nobody else got to see; things that nobody knew about. I had to face the situation for what it was and instead of trying to change anything about it, I walked away from my dad, the farm, and some of the family that didn't agree with breaking up the family facade.

Not only did I step away from family, but I also stepped away from what I call the Midwestern Mindset which is centered around limiting beliefs, close-mindedness, working hard for little reward, taking pride in how you look on the outside without it matching on the inside, and loyalty over health or safety.

Now, there are many amazing things about the Midwest that I love and am proud of. And there is an underbelly to this culture that no one talks about but there isn't a way to break the cycle if we all stay silent about it and struggle alone. I have even been questioned about why I need to share all this. In fact, in the Midwest, it may be considered 'airing your dirty laundry' but that still lives in the context of secrecy, not accountability. I decided years ago that this *was not okay.* What was happening in my home was not okay and that I would not allow it.

As I've shared, even as young as five years old, I knew better than to let my dad viciously attack my mom and just watch her struggle. As messed up as it might seem, there were times when I would manipulate the argument to turn the tides against me. I would take on his aggression so that he would leave my mom alone and give her a break. I have always been willing to step into the middle of injustice and that is what I plan to do. I plan to break the patterns and cycles of abuse. I plan to intervene in the injustices bestowed upon us by previous generations. I believe we have been disabled in many ways by lack of education, particularly in the area of financial literacy, which I think is its own category of abuse established by our culture. I find it unfair that so many people have been set up to fail in our economy and I have set out to transform that. This book is freedom for me, releasing the burdens of my past, one word at a time. I hope to help you do the same.

As we continue to grow together throughout this book, I want you to know that no matter how much or how little you relate to my personal or professional story, consider your own emotional scars. Consider how they have shaped your identity, behaviors, and life. As I tell my story, consider how the way you grew up impacted your circumstances, manifestations, and outcomes.

I constantly look out for how my upbringing is dictating my actions, reactions, words, feelings, and choices. These little things about us become big things as we operate unconsciously in the world. If we want a fair shot at an abundant and unlimited future, when we break away from our past, we must acknowledge how it impacted us and focus on healing it as well.

Breaking away from the people, places, and things that hold you back are an important step in heading towards a new, healthier, more abundant life. I really wish I didn't have to say that, yet I do. There will be people who don't want you to win. You can stay small forever fighting to bring those people with you toward your dreams, but the cost is staying where you are or dragging them along. You are going to have to go out on a few limbs and some of those branches will feel really shaky while you are out there.

I stood up for myself. I stood for ending generational abuse. I took that stand so that my daughter would know what it looks like to have a mom who is healthy and empowered. I did it with the commitment to grow a family who didn't have to heal from generational trauma. I took that risk and my life is unrecognizable because of it. It is because I have made it to the other side of that fire that I feel qualified to teach you how to take these steps for yourself.

I know what it feels like to be scared to death to stand in my truth; to stand in the authenticity of who I am. As I go on to teach investing in financial freedom, I want you to know this is more about you than it is about money. Standing in your truth is investing. It is investing in yourself. It's betting on you. If you wouldn't bet on yourself, you can bet no one else will want to either.

I know what it's like to not be able to depend on people. I know what it feels like to have to turn away from relationships that weren't healthy for me anymore. I know what it feels like to do the scariest things I would never want to do for the sake of a prosperous future. I know what it feels like to lose more money than I had ever made combined. I know what it feels like to be depressed, fighting with the deepest, darkest, life-ending thoughts. I know what it feels like to be a fighter, fighting for a better quality of life.

But you know what? I also know what it feels like to make a million dollars in a year when all the odds are stacked against me. I now know what it feels like to take my family on luxury vacations. I know what it feels like to own my own property. I know what it feels like to provide homes and jobs for my community. I know what it feels like to achieve financial freedom.

Beyond the wildly wonderful things I have created materially, I also know what it is like to live in my purpose. I know what it is like to heal and forgive. I know the gift of letting go of my past and grabbing on to my future. I know what it is like to stand in my power, and I will spend this entire book, and my entire life, teaching you to do the same.

Chapter 6

Become Willing to Dream

"A lot of us learned it was selfish to want too much but I am here to tell you that you get what you ask for and if you don't get clear about what you ask for, you will get something close but just a bit off. This is the power of asking."

Okay, friend. You have learned a lot about me in the last few chapters and we are going to start talking a bit more about you and our journey together throughout the rest of these pages. I am sure the financial freedom portion of this book's title caught your attention, and I am here to help you do that. When I say wealth, I mean well-rounded wealth, which includes your well-being. When I talk about manifestations, yes, I mean material manifestations, but I also mean the manifestation of your wholeness and happiness. I am talking about you living an abundant life in every way possible; success in any way you define and desire.

To those of you feeling limited in what you can create, I relate. If you question your potential or what's possible for you, I get it. What I know about you is that you bought this book because there is a very faithful part of you, tucked away deep inside, that believes in yourself. I also understand there are layers of disbelief piled on top of that faithful one. I get you on a soul level. I had to learn to honor my own soul to get where I am today in order to be able to walk with you on your journey.

In the next chapter, I am going to dive into my favorite conversation: financial freedom. Before that, I want to offer you a few things to consider about your past, present, and future that affect your manifestation abilities. I will share in entirety with more detail to help you produce measurable results in your life, but I would like to start from the top, down.

To call in anything you desire, it must start from your dreams and visions. You cannot manifest if you are not willing or able to dream and visualize. Everything that has ever come into form was first a thought. So, remember, thoughts become things. This is true across the board, so becoming more responsible with your thoughts will bring more desirable things into your life. So, let's start thinking with more focus and intention.

Let's elevate far above your physical life, as if you were watching your own existence from the sky, maybe even from space. If we zoomed out and looked from that far back, the perspective would be much wider. This expansive view would give you the vantage point of making bigger declarations for your life than just wanting the next new, shiny 'thing' or making the next dollar.

We want to start with the experience you want to be having in life. When it's all over, how will you want your story to be told? How do you want to be remembered? Consider some of the overarching themes you desire for your life. For me, I want my experience of life to be abundant, fun, wild, and adventurous. I want to be remembered as generous, kind, passionate, compassionate, hilarious, thoughtful, and inclusive. I want to leave a legacy of love and light.

Of course, if I am living this kind of life experience, you can imagine that material wealth will be a natural byproduct of that. For some, wealth is living below or within their means. To others, that means comfort. For others, that is living in luxury, and for others, that is extravagance. You get to decide how much is enough and what success means to you. As long as you are living *your* definition of wealthy, then you *are* wealthy. Riches can be measured in endless ways.

Very soon after I gave up the dream of inheriting my family farm, I released a lot of pressure I was putting on myself and my imagination was activated in a new way. I started to consider what I wanted for myself, my life, and my own family. When I started having dreams of my own, they flooded in *fast*.

That said, I want to share with you something that I would have wanted my younger self to know. I am about to tell you something that I teach my children and would teach anyone I care about: You know those dreams that tug at your heart strings?

You know those visions you see in your mind's eye, that you wish you could have? You know those experiences you wish you could have, the lifestyle you wish you could live, the work you wish you could do, the car you wish you could drive, and the family and spouse you wish you could have?

I'm going to let you in on a secret.

You can have those dreams.

All of them.

I will do you one better. Close your eyes and imagine those dreams for a moment. All of them. All the life you can dream up. All the manifestations you could ever hope for and take a deep breath in. Envision them coming true and exhale with a smile.

Now, think even bigger. Imagine all you just visualized came true and go beyond that. What would be next? Dream with even more clarity. Consider the questions below with detail and permission to dream. Now, this permission part is important. Many of us were trained not to dream too big. A lot of us learned it was selfish to want too much but I am here to tell you that you get what you ask for, and if you don't get clear about what you ask for, you will get something close but just a bit off. This is the power of asking.

When I broke away from my family's dream and started having my own, my life blossomed. The more it happened, the clearer and more committed I got. I encourage you to dream bigger and use your wild imagination. The days of being dampened by outside influences are over. Permission to dream, my friend! Now, tell me…

What kind of house will you live in? What kind of property will you live on? Will it be in the country? City? Internationally somewhere? Floating from city to city, country to country every few years? Will you stay near your hometown? Will you travel the world? Will you have kids? What kind of clothes will you wear? What kind of work will you do? What kind of friends will you have? What kind of foods will you eat? What kind of books will you read? What kinds of activities will you enjoy? How much money will you have in the bank? What will you spend your money on? What will you invest in? When will you retire? What will you do in your retirement?

We are going to just keep getting better with visualization and manifestation throughout this book and I want to normalize something about when we start practicing dreaming. This life you are visualizing might feel too big for the level of faith you currently have. At first, this can create a feeling of despair, hopelessness, or even envy of those who already have something you want. This is a natural part of the process. I say this because it is the dreaming that will stretch you into the person that can have the dream, so never stop visualizing. You can close the gap between you and what you want, if you are willing to acknowledge what you want in the first place. It is all a part of the process.

My word of encouragement is that anything that wasn't a true desire will naturally fade away over time but the desires that are authentic to your soul and purpose will remain true. Those are the dreams that stick. Pin up pictures of those dreams. Put them on a vision board somewhere you will see every day. Tape them to your mirror or to the wall in your bedroom. Post them up in your office. Put them up to keep them at the front of your mind and hold your focus. It is your focused attention that pulls your desires closer and will inspire you to take aligned steps toward those manifestations daily.

Throughout this book, I will teach you concepts about money

and manifestation that help you release the old to welcome the new. This is all a practice in trust that you are an endlessly abundant being participating in the circulation of goods, not a hoarder of them. As you become a powerful manifestor, you will also find that you want more over time. That is okay, too. It is a natural law of evolution. This is all a healthy part of the process. Consider it 'elevation.' From a higher vantage point, you can see more of the horizon. You can see more of what you want out of life, and it is okay to go for it.

I want to encourage you to keep going even if it feels uncomfortable. You might feel loss but there is a gain coming from the release. The discomfort is a sign that you are stretching into a new belief system. I want to shine the light of hope into your life so that you will wake up from any games you are playing that disempower or even disable you from manifesting your wildest dreams. This is the time that you get to acknowledge that you are willing to step out of your comfort zone to go for something greater.

In this next chapter, I am going to share with you exactly how I did that in my life. I can tell you, it wasn't very comfortable. Sometimes it was downright scary, but I would do it all a million times over again knowing what I know now. I would do it a million times because it has earned me millions; money in the bank and energetic abundance beyond measure. That is why I want to encourage you to dream big; because you can have it all, no matter how you measure your 'millions.'

Chapter 7

An Entrepreneur
at Heart

*"I believed that freedom of all kinds was meant for me and anyone who
was willing to go for it."*

I was an entrepreneur before I knew what an entrepreneur was.
My first endeavor began on the elementary school playground at the
age of nine. As soon as I learned how to sew, it was game on.

It was the 90's and scrunchies were all the craze. My mom had
heaps of extra fabric and rounds of elastic bands piled up in her
sewing cabinets from old projects. I was finally tall enough to operate the presser foot and hold down the fabric without running over
my finger with the needle, which I had once done to my mom.
Sorry, Mom!

Once I was finally able to sew on my own, she taught me how
to make scrunchies. My brain ran as fast as that sewing machine.
I figured all I had to do was put them together, slip them into my
backpack for school, wait for the bell to ring for recess, and peddle
them on the playground. No one told me to. It just made perfect
sense to me.

I sold them for whatever quarters, dimes, and nickels my friends
had in their pockets. I also traded for marbles because those were a

big thing then, too. I made scrunchies of all different colors and patterns and they sold as quickly as I made them. The girls loved them and I loved making them. I also loved making money.

I grew up staring at posters on classroom walls that read, 'Dream Big' and 'Reach for the Stars.' I felt like I could do anything I put my mind to. I remember always having a desire to not only be financially stable but to have a lot of money. The problem with that early on was there weren't a lot of people I knew in my area talking about money as much as I wondered about it. I was always looking to make a buck.

Another beginner venture of mine was candy sales. I was one of the only kids who went trick-or-treating on Halloween to make a profit, instead of to eat all the candy. While trick-or-treating in whatever ridiculously unfortunate costume my mom had sewn up for me to wear, I would happily collect whatever Halloween candy I could fit into my plastic orange pumpkin. When my friends and I were all done for the night, I would only eat a few pieces and save the rest. I knew that in a few short weeks, I was going to make my profit.

I lived in the gateway to the middle of nowhere, surrounded by the woods and valleys of southwest Wisconsin, but one thing I could count on was deer season. Deer hunting time was the biggest draw of the year, and it was also the time of the biggest annual gathering on our farm. It brought out the burliest of men and women for seven days straight and every year, my candy stand was a big hit.

In true Wisconsin fashion, hunters and guests would line up their famous crock pots of chili and make bets on who had the spiciest snack sticks and the best cheese. You would find me right alongside the food table with my candy table. I would sort and organize all the candy by size and tape a sign with their respective prices on it. Everyone would clean out the change trays in their trucks to appease my entrepreneurial endeavors and put a big smile on the face of an eager little farm girl in her business pursuits.

Making money made sense to me which is why I never understood why more of the people around me didn't seem to value it as much as I did. I had not heard the term 'financial freedom' until my young adult years. In my home, most of the financial discussions revolved around paying bills, figuring out what we could afford, what was off limits, and yearly taxes, which was all kept in a giant ledger book that my mom tracked. I could tell very early that money was a taboo topic based on the way my parents did their bookkeeping in secret. It wasn't a conversation we kids were involved in. I usually listened in the way that I overheard their fights: through the grate in the floor.

I felt inspired by those posters at school but found myself confused when adults would say that I should not worry about making money. It didn't make sense when they would make statements like *money doesn't matter* and *money isn't everything*. It seemed like a contradiction to me, as though you could 'Dream Big' and 'Reach for the Stars' as long as you didn't go after making a lot of money.

This seemed true at school and at home. We had what we needed and not much more. We did what was financially necessary. We were not financially educated by our teachers or our parents. In the Midwest, unless you grew up in an entrepreneurial or wealth-conscious family, you probably hadn't heard much about taxes, financial statements, credit scores, and cash flow. Other topics not covered in the classroom or at our dinner table were types of investing or having multiple streams of income. I would venture to say the most informative a finance conversation may have gotten was contributing to a retirement fund.

It was such a taboo topic that many of the beliefs about money that I acquired over the years were unspoken. It was often the conversation that was not had that made me even more curious about money. It was the way people got uptight about money that made me pay attention. I could sense the energy shift when a conversation was about finances, or someone was avoiding a conversation about finances. There was a certain kind of avoidance that felt uncomfortable.

The other side of that very confusing coin were sayings and beliefs like *money doesn't buy happiness* or that *the best things in life are free,* which made it seem as though making money meant that you were a bad person who didn't care about the simple joys of life. Throughout my life, I concluded that you either do what you love, or you make money, but not both. For decades, these beliefs were just the truth to me. A few other truths that I adopted as my own were that you work hard for your money, money is hard earned, hard won, and hard to get.

There were a lot of assumptions about 'rich folk' that were downright judgmental. I was taught to think that people who lived lavish lives of ease and comfort somehow lived dishonestly. They must have gotten their wealth by inheritance, greed, or cheating the system somehow, as if they were lazy, entitled, and spoiled. There was a sense of jealousy, judgment, or rejection of those living a wealthy lifestyle.

For example, we had a relative that always drove Cadillac cars. I remember him pulling onto our farm to visit my dad in his shiny, white, luxury vehicles and it would always give me butterflies in my stomach. There I would be, standing in front of our shed, playing basketball by myself in oversized hand-me-down clothes from my sister; dirty from helping feed steers and doing chores. I could feel the stark difference between his luxury vehicle and nice clothes and my dad's overalls and boots. There was an unspoken tension in his presence.

Standing there in front of a shabby excuse for a basketball hoop, with a dirty ball in my hand, I would watch his sparkling white Cadillac roll down our dusty farm driveway. Even though I loved farming and enjoyed the simple life, there was always something alluring and intriguing about what our cousin did that he could afford such nice cars. One visit, I asked him what kind of job he had.

"Real estate investing," he responded with a proud smile. I could tell he loved what he did and that gave me more butterflies. I had no idea what real estate investing was but I could tell it made a lot more money than farming did. I was intrigued but didn't really look into it any further at the time. I was still very young and more interested in that dusty basketball going in the hoop, but the thought never left me.

Another thing that never left me was the sight of that big white Cadillac rolling down our drive. That sparkle sparked something in me; a desire for nice things. But I never mentioned that around our household. I kept my desire to make a lot of money to myself because of how much I had overheard that it was selfish to want to be rich.

I have noticed that something very subtle happens when you are raised to have a 'blue collar' mindset; you identify with it. In my years of growth, I have seen that this definitely happens in other cultures as well. It may just have a different name. In many cultures, it is bad to just be okay with receiving abundantly. It is bad to be okay with more. It is frowned upon to want nice things and have high standards. These cultural and societal standards shape how we act and who we become.

If it is all we ever know, we may adopt those beliefs without recognizing them as beliefs. They are *the way the world works.* They are *the way money works.* Life *is what it is* and things *are the way they are,* not to be challenged or changed. As a result, this becomes an identity, and in the Midwest, it is a noble one. You are 'salt of the earth' if you are kind and modest. You are considered nice if you act meek and humble and you are bad, wrong, arrogant, materialistic, and shallow if you value money or prioritize making it in more efficient ways.

I happened to become one of the casualties of that modest Midwest mindset that taught us it was good and right to go to school and get good grades, so you can go to college and get a secure job working for someone else. I went as far as earning a bachelor's and master's degree in education to achieve that American standard of achievement.

I graduated from high school in the bottom half of my class. Even though I was told I wasn't going to make it at a four-year university, I went anyway. There was a lot of talk about doing what you love and that the rest would take care of itself, so I got my degree in agriculture education and a minor in biology. I did, however, have a blast earning a third degree in being the life of the party at my rural Midwestern college.

I loved agriculture. It was what I knew so I went with it, not really caring about what kind of money I would make or even really nailing down what kind of occupation I would have in the future. I made some awesome friends and had the time of my life along the way. I remember thinking after graduation, *this is it! I finally have my degrees! I am golden. I am all set.* However, after the parties dwindled and everyone went their separate ways to start their careers, reality started to settle in.

I reasoned that going for a life in agriculture would be fine because I had so much experience in the field, even before earning my degree. I had traveled quite a bit of the country performing a wide range of agricultural jobs. From picking strawberries to herding cattle to building fences to surveying crops, I really felt like I had done it all in the 'ag' world and it gave me a lot of confidence in the field.

I remember being so excited when I landed my first high school teaching job. I aced the interview. I knocked their socks off with my candor, charm, and high energy. I was awarded the high school ag teacher position at $32,500 per year. I made it. I did what I was supposed to do. I got 'the good' job. I didn't really think anything of the salary because I was so happy to have landed the job at a pretty sweet high school.

I worked in the ag field for quite a while, but it took me becoming a teacher to realize that those jobs didn't make much money compared to the cost of living. It didn't occur to me until after college when I was paying my own bills that I had to actually pay attention to the money coming in. I knew the life I imagined for myself, but no one taught me to figure out how much that lifestyle would cost. This was a rude awakening for me. All my life, I was trained to be a great employee; to be a rule follower. I wasn't trained to crunch numbers. I completed all the steps I thought I was supposed to and it felt like it cost me more than it made me; financially or otherwise.

Sure, the extra spending money from those ag jobs was great as a teen or college kid but it was when my adult expenses started to outweigh my adult income that the statement money isn't everything or money can't buy happiness seemed like a crock of shit. Who came up with that idea anyway? I was struggling to just afford my basics, let alone be able to do anything extra. I would look at my bank account balance and there wasn't a whole lot left to enjoy life with. Suddenly, I needed my degree to earn me more money than I was currently bringing in and 'getting a good job' didn't seem like such a great idea anymore.

Right around when teaching started, it became very apparent that my college car was done for, and I needed a new car. It was the one my parents had got me and at this point, I had to drive with the windows down and the heat cranked just to cool down the engine. Remember that hard-working, blue-collar mentality I mentioned? We drive our cars 'till the wheels fall off' because that's just what you do to get your money's worth. Well, the wheels didn't fall off this one, but I feared the engine was going to explode at any minute.

So, I did what any self-respecting, highly educated, young adult would do after they land their first job. I bought a brand-new car at full price. I drove my rumbly, blumby beater into the dealership with steam coming out the hood. I jumped out and proudly declared that I was there to buy a brand new, white, stylish Pontiac G6 with a sun-roof and air conditioning. It was no Cadillac, but it was perfect for me. Most importantly, no more overheating beater.

Then, the payments began. Then, I started noticing my income wasn't matching my expenses. Then, a couple short months into my first teaching job, I slipped a disc in my back, barely able to sit in my brand-new car for the thirteen-mile drive to work and back. I kept working by standing all day, because sitting was too painful, until I could finally receive a microdiscectomy surgery and get off the three most intense pain-killing and numbing drugs on the market. Then, the medical bills came. Then, insurance bills came. After all that, my back didn't hurt from a slipped disc. It hurt from the weight of those bills.

It only seemed to get worse when I went to dinner during a girls' weekend away. I was on such a tight budget for my groceries and one night, my friends and I went to a fancy fondue restaurant. When my bill came to the table and it was equal to what I would've needed for a whole month of my groceries, I wanted to puke up all the awesome food and drinks I had just enjoyed. I was noticeably uncomfortable, staring out the window the whole way home feeling that food weigh me down like a bowling ball in my stomach…or at least a month's worth of groceries in there.

That was about the time when I started to feel envious of my friends who seemed to be making more money than I was. I didn't really know what they earned for an income, but I could clearly tell they were doing better than me. Even though money was a taboo topic, I worked up the courage to ask one of my best friend's what kind of money she was making. She had landed some sweet sales jobs out of college, was shopping at luxury boutiques, and traveling to lavish locations regularly. She shared that after her yearly bonus, she was bringing in around $100,000 per year. I was floored. Her answer nearly took my breath away.

I tried not to look downright shocked, but I was. I wasn't jealous anymore; I was completely taken aback at the staggering difference in our jobs and income. When I heard what she made, I was upset that I had gone into teaching and not into sales. I was so upset that I had followed what society had told me to do by going into a field that would allow me to do what I loved because people always told me that the money didn't matter. "Just do what you love" sounded like a complete scam at this point. I am pretty sure I could have made more money sticking to my Halloween candy sales at that point.

I will share more as we dive into part two of this book, but I left that teaching job and moved onto another agriculture job, which didn't put me much further ahead, but it was a step. It was a step further away from the Midwest mindset of minimizing the true value of money. It helped me start considering what else was out there and when I met my husband, Noah, he really opened my eyes to what was possible.

Without giving away a spoiler alert on a later chapter, meeting Noah started a chain reaction of heading toward financial freedom on the fast track. I had found a sprinter who I could run with, and we did. This started to transform everything. It took years to unravel the fabric of my upbringing, but I knew I had to step away from a modest money mindset and become okay with being an entrepreneur at heart. I knew I had to become okay with my love and appreciation of money. I had to reach deep down and bring back the hopeful, pig-tail-wearing, scrunchie-making and Halloween candy salesgirl.

Leaving the workforce as an employee was thrilling but still took many years of growth after that to really reach financial freedom. Every year, I was stretching myself further to reach my goal. I was determined to live a different life than the one I came from. I just knew in my bones that living a great life was possible and I was determined to find out how to prove that life could be better than average. I believed that freedom of all kinds was meant for me and anyone who is willing to go for it. I wanted to be free. I wanted to live the life I'd always dreamed of. I didn't want to be held back by anything.

In this book, I will be sharing more of our stories, our messes, and our methodologies in order to help you reach for financial freedom while also avoiding burnout and exhaustion. I want to help you reach financial freedom in an inspired way so that when you get to say the words, "I am a millionaire" for the first time, you actually celebrate your pants off and jump around hooting and hollering around your house. This isn't a get-rich-at-all-costs kind of guide. This is a follow-your-heart-to-your-fortune kind of manual.

I've spent most of my life proving people and myself wrong. That has taken me to some pretty fantastic heights but also some really heavy lows. As we move forward together, I am going to teach you how to make your millions while also avoiding the blunders of being bullheaded and stubborn, like I can sometimes be. What I want you to know is that making your money can be fun and exciting if you are also ready and willing to heal the wounding of your past, take proper care of yourself, respect money for the amazing tool that it is, and celebrate along the way.

I hope you're ready to dive in and go after the things in your life that make your heart sing. You get to manifest all the goodness you desire. All the money and financial freedom you desire. It is possible. I am here to prove that and that is what you are here for too! The abundance life has to offer is here for the taking. Let's get it.

Part 2

Chapter 8

Fighters Fight

"Instead of staying in a situation to fight against it, I walked away to pursue a more peaceful path, even if that left a few people behind."

As I write this, my kids, who woke up at five-thirty in the morning, are crawling up and down off my lap while I type at a small desk in the corner of our kitchen. My husband is feeding them their breakfast behind me. I figured that I could get up at five and have two hours to write on this early Sunday morning. Their Mom radar went off earlier than expected today and that's okay. I love listening to them singing "Old MacDonald" in the background as I write to you.

When I ponder my life, I feel a wave of gratitude that I am giving them my childhood dreams here at our own farmstead; one infused with love. As a kid, I always hoped and prayed to have kids. I would envision raising them to see what healthy love and marriage looks like. I wanted to give them the experience of being raised on a farm with great memories and that's exactly what I am doing. A little spoiler alert, I am a master manifestor and will teach you more about that in the second half of this book.

Noah and I have goals to own lots of acreage of farmland with hills and trees to ride horses, like I did when I was a kid. It's something I'm excited to provide for my kids because it's a way of life that I love. They are ages three and five at the time of writing this book and already love farm life. It brings me such joy to share the treasures of the land with them. I want to raise them in a healthy environment with good memories, happy times, and loving relationships.

So much of how I grew up influenced who I married and how I am raising my children. I worked for years, and still do to dismantle the effects of trauma, heal, and live empowered. Abuse caused so much damage in my life that I vowed to myself to do better, end the cycles, and lay a foundation for something unrecognizable. In many ways, having a daughter and raising her well is redemption for a younger version of myself who grew up in turmoil. I promised myself and God that my daughter, Tesla and son, Jace, would never have to see what I've seen. They haven't and I will do anything I can to prevent that.

I have witnessed the damage that abuse can cause, and I feel so blessed that God guided Noah and I to each other to build our beautiful lives together. What I witnessed in my youth taught me a lot about what not to do, but also showed me how to find a great marriage partner. I never take for granted how my story has developed. There are far too many kids that repeat the generational trauma by finding a spouse like their parents. This carries on the pain and suffering. I always knew I didn't want to contribute to the cycle of abuse.

When I sit and watch my life play out, like I am right now, typing and hearing "e-i-e-i-o" yodeled from the kitchen, I think about what I want my children to learn. Little people are so amazing. They are such blank slates that you get to help grow into big people. It is a mind-blowing process, and it shocks me almost every day. They are beautiful. They are full of life, and I want them to feel loved and supported by their daddy and I.

I want them to learn to go for things they want and believe in. I want to teach them ethics, integrity, and faith. I want them to be loving, caring, compassionate, and know what it means to be there for others. I want to teach them to love and value themselves just as much. I want to teach them to dream big and chase those dreams wildly. I could probably go on and on about all the hopes and dreams I have for my children, but I pray they feel limitless in what they can achieve in this lifetime.

Something that I have really struggled with is how early on I raised them to not know their grandpa (my dad), or to have limited visitations with my mom. When it came to this part of parenthood, this wasn't how I imagined raising kids. I didn't imagine keeping them from each other. My daughter used to run around saying she had two grandmas and one papa. She didn't realize she had two grandfathers.

It would cut deep when I would hear her say that, so innocently. It hurt. I was unsure how to explain my family to her. I didn't want to go there because I didn't want to introduce the concepts of fighting, arguing, disagreements, and manipulation to her. Early on in her life, it was simpler to let her believe she only had one papa, but it didn't take away the sting. I didn't know what to say when her cousins mentioned going to their grandpa's farm to ride horses, and my daughter realized that was her grandpa's farm too and she had never been there. It sucked. It was hard. It was complicated but I couldn't be available for that situation anymore.

My gingerbread dreams crumbled one graham cracker crumb after another until I had a pile of powdered mess to either clean up or walk away from. I had to face the facts that the dynamics between my parents and I were something I would have to take charge of, for the health and well-being of my own growing family. When I realized my vision for my life held unrealistic expectations of my parents, I had to let those dreams die. I had to force myself to move on. Now, we are establishing our own farm. I am building my own life and it will be one void of abuse. I would never choose this for my family but in the end, I had to.

I have spent a lot of this book being really raw and real about what went on behind closed doors at our house and on our farm, the one my children haven't been to yet. I have mostly given you a pretty vulnerable look into my world, but you haven't gotten the full view just yet.

The fact of the matter was that growing up, I was one hundred percent a daddy's girl. I felt like I had different access to him than my other siblings. We had a special bond. I looked up to him and he looked down at me as his baby girl. There are a few factors that tied us closer together like both being the youngest children in our families and having a special love of the family farm. We are also both stubborn and determined. I followed his example and developed a very strong work ethic and wasn't afraid to bale hay and build fences. I was always trying to keep up with him and he let me tag along. I am not too sure if he would ever openly acknowledge that I was his favorite but if I had to guess, I would be willing to make that bet.

Some of my favorite childhood memories are with my dad. He really nurtured my love of farming, horseback riding, and hunting, so he supported all my 4-H and school ventures. Both of my parents were great at being at my extracurriculars and showing their support that way. My parents came to all of my choir/band concerts, FFA banquets, and cross country or track meets. My dad would also take me to steer check-ins to weigh them in. I have so many fond memories of quality time with my dad, like when we would sit together in the deer blind. I remember feeling so special spending one on one time with him. Even though we had our challenges as a family, I have always felt grateful for my parents' presence in my life. I am well aware that so many children go without parents and siblings from a very early age and I am just so appreciative for what I did have and the good times I remember.

It was a personal favorite when he included me in his ventures. He would take me on 'parts runs' to go get new tractor parts or welding equipment for the farm and I just loved hopping up into his pick-up truck to go for a ride with dad. It usually meant we got to stop somewhere for lunch where I would always order a grilled cheese sandwich with a pickle and chips. I can see it as clearly as if it were yesterday, Dad in his overalls on a humid Wisconsin summer day with the windows down and the radio up. I remember feeling so special riding along, the farmer's daughter. I especially loved tagging along and saying hi to his friends along the way. I enjoyed overhearing grown-up conversation and feeling included. I knew he loved me and was proud of me.

I also learned so much about our area as he'd drive around telling stories of how he used to drive the milk truck in our township when he was in college. He'd describe what each farm used to look like and tell me about each family who milked cows. He'd talk about what it was like in the milk truck to be driving on the steep roads in the wintertime on the ice and snow. He would reminisce about the hustle and bustle of every little farm getting ready for the day; those barns with forty cows chewing their cud and the family all working together to get the chores done. He loved seeing the glow of the warm barn lights through the glass block windows at night when it was cold outside, knowing that it was warm there. I miss hearing those stories. I miss those good times together. It was those stories that grew my love for the land I came from and the multiple generations that lived there before me.

Claiming to be the favorite of four children may seem like a bold-faced lie based on the way that I have introduced him to you so far in this book, but breaking away had much more to do with my mental health than our relationship. You see, from a very early age I was empathic and very intuitive. I was the one to jump in between my parents. I was the one asking them to work together and talk it out. I was always trying to fix and mend things in our immediate family because I wanted to see them love each other as much as I loved them.

I would often call him out on his bullshit act because I had a sense of his heart, but so often, he chose anger and violence. I could see beyond his rage. I vividly remember yelling during his fits "this is not who you are!" trying to pull him back to reality.

When I was younger, this was okay. I was young enough that it worked in my favor. For example, he wouldn't give me a hard time when I would hide his Swisher Sweet Cigars under his truck seat so he couldn't find them. He knew I didn't want him to smoke so he cut me some slack. I knew he could always sense I was looking out for him.

Growing up, we had a lot of fun together because we 'got' each other. I felt loved by him and had a sense of unique connection. It made me feel valued and proud. It also gave me a sense of entitlement when it came to my dad. I often didn't hold back when I thought he needed to hear that he was being an asshole. Once I grew up, he didn't want my unsolicited feedback or backlash. As I got older, this built tension between us. So often, too often, my attempts to diffuse his anger didn't work. I usually fueled the fire. I would get to him because I saw through him, and he didn't want to be held accountable. This became harder on my heart over the years. I was running out of energy for the fight.

Something that I want to make really clear is that, deep down, I love my dad. I love him a lot and to walk away and stay away from him for years on end was one of the most challenging choices of my life. I had to continue to make that choice every day that I did it. Particularly every year, when my sister would come home from living out of the country and she'd stay on our family farm. For a long time, I would make the exception and go home to visit my sister and dad and I would predictably have a blowup and I would leave as angry as ever. It was especially hard because I was the 'optimistic victim' who would think *enough time had passed, maybe he changed* so I would go back. I finally went back enough times without a positive change that I was forced to accept what it was.

I mentioned how I was always the one to jump in to fix things, but I had finally tried and failed enough that I also became the only sibling to fully cut ties for seven years. Some might wonder how you go from being the favorite to the black sheep, but it seems pretty obvious to me. The level of hurt and distance created comes from the level of love and connection. The disappointment of the situation was too much to bear to keep going back to the toxicity of manipulation. The only way to heal fully was to give myself space to heal and while healing, I had to maintain a separation because going back would rip that wound wide open again and each time, it got deeper.

I love my dad but somewhere along the line, I had to decide that

I love myself too. I love myself enough to walk away and simply love him from afar. I had to give up my own dream of the happily-ever-after farm and it took me leaving to lift the fog that kept me going back. Another thing my dad and I had in common was hiding our true selves with overly active charisma, humor, and jolliness. While there is definitely an authentically fun, light-hearted version of me, I learned very early how to put on a happy face to mask pain and suffering behind the facade.

This lesson was a major factor when deciding to write my book because I don't think enough people talk about family dynamics on a mainstream level. It is sort of taboo to be open and honest about what we face with family but the more we talk about it, the more we find out how much shit everyone is dealing with.

The more I have shared my story over the years, the more feedback I have gotten about how much people relate to me and my life. I have heard countless similar stories of abuse. They have had to escape domestic violence situations, end relationships, actively heal from trauma, and attempt to create their own life and their own definition of normal. It was a huge adjustment for me to finally give up on my dad and walk away because it was so far from what I knew as a little girl.

My dad gave us a great life in so many ways. He inspired my love of the Rockies and for each of our four high school graduations, we got to go on a family vacation to Florida to celebrate. We had a lot of great experiences and memories in life, but like I mentioned in an earlier chapter, it can be hard to remember the good when the bad was so traumatizing. There is a popular analogy to this that someone can get ten compliments but will remember and dwell on one insult. This is how it felt when I thought about my childhood, but it didn't actually eliminate all the good we experienced. In so many ways, I am grateful to my parents for giving me such an amazing life.

What I did learn at an early age is that if I wanted to see change, if I wanted to make a difference, I had to do it myself. If I saw injustice happening in our household back then, I tried to do what

I could as a kid, which was jump in the middle. It took me until my adulthood to realize that I wasn't going to be able to stop what was happening in my house. When I was young, I was dependent on my family. I needed them and things never got so bad that it occurred to me to run away and the domestic violence in our house was never reported. So, it wasn't until age eighteen that anything would change for us kids.

In the long run, I have become grateful for my story because my upbringing has made me who I am; a fighter. I have survived some incredible situations in my life that have taught me how to overcome all sorts of adversity. I can remember times when I threw punches I never knew I had in me. I didn't know I could punch so hard. I was a trained fighter from five to twenty-three years old, and I know that it turned me into a resilient woman as a wife, mother, business owner, and so much more. I don't throw punches anymore, but I certainly get up every single time life tries to knock me down.

If breaking barriers, problem solving, and proving people wrong were actual talents in the Miss America competition, they would've been mine. Being raised to fight taught me to fight for what I think is right. It taught me how to go for my dreams and not stop when it gets discouraging. I learned year after year to show up for what I believe in, hold the vision, and go for all that is possible. I credit my fighter's mentality for my incredible success in life.

I carried these amazing talents into our business when I started real estate investing, building homes, and being a real estate broker. When we first started our real estate investing company, we were just engaged. We went to our very first real estate investing class in Chicago exactly one year prior to our wedding weekend. It was an exciting time for us.

Many people in our lives were nervous about us starting a business before we were married. We were advised against it for fear that we would get ourselves in over our heads. We were discouraged by the only real estate investor in my family. Yeah, my Cadillac cousin. He would give us copies of the Wall Street Journal that headlined grim forecasts for the future of real estate. We didn't listen. We started our business anyway.

Soon after that first class, we started our first LLC, and the journey began. At our wedding on the family farm one year later, my sister gave the Matron of Honor speech and said that if Noah and I could successfully launch a real estate investing business in a recession, we could do anything. It seemed like everyone raised their wine glasses just a little higher than usual because it was such a worthy toast. We had really defied the odds.

In our years of life, business, and marriage, my fighter's mentality has gotten us into some crazy stuff, but it has also brought us crazy awesome results. We had blind ambition. We played full out with our passion and youthful optimism. We believed we were going to set the business world on fire with our determination and our charm and we pretty much did.

I will never forget the day that we were, yet again, upleveling in our business ventures and I asked Noah for his feedback on making a substantial investment on building our support team. I was leveling up in new ways that scared both of us and I needed confirmation that this was the next right move. Deep down, I knew it was, but I stood for our team. I value our partnership in everything, so hearing from him meant a lot and what I heard this time just about melted my whole heart.

"Babe, if it weren't for you, I'd still just be driving my pickup truck around landscaping. Everything we have is because of your big, bold moves. I trust you. This is a good move. Let's do it," he said with his sweet smile.

I will share more in the next few chapters about all of the ups and downs in our relationship and partnership, but this was certainly a life peak moment that set me, us, free to climb higher. It set me free to unleash the boldest part of me to show up for this book and the education we are offering to those ready to make millions and make a difference doing it. It has always been my blind, bold ambition that has taken me higher and further in life. It is the fighter in me, but instead of being bullheaded like in my youth, I am clear and faithful as I forge unpaved paths to freedom.

I am going to help you forge your own path to freedom as we continue on together. I recognize that not everyone might have something to prove. Not everyone was raised to fight, defend, and overcome. Some folks have a lighter approach, or one with more finesse. I can be a bit more bull-in-a-China-shop, but I respect that some like to play it safer than I do, and some are also more risk averse than I am. That doesn't make either approach good, bad, right, or wrong. Everyone's approach is valid and important. What is most important is having an active awareness about yourself.

What happened behind closed doors impacted how I showed up in life. I concluded and internalized some core beliefs that shaped so much of my identity and future. When I was unconsciously a fighter, I was throwing punches at my dad. When I consciously applied my fighter mentality, I used my grit to face challenges in life. This is a big difference that produced very different outcomes. I am grateful I was able to mature past the angry attacker with something to prove and evolved into a businesswoman, wife, and mother, with a life to live. I want to live my best life and I want that for you, too.

What I would like to do at this point of the book is have you take a much closer look at who and how you are. I would like you to consider how your upbringing has impacted you. I want to provide you an opportunity to take a look into your own history to identify how your past has shaped the way you turned out and how you deal with life. Take a moment's break from reading and consider getting out your favorite notebook to journal on these questions:

# Self Reflection

What are some of the most pivotal moments of your childhood?

What beliefs did you inherit from your family that you didn't realize are not actually yours?

What identities took shape in your childhood that are no longer necessary in your adulthood? Can they go now? Can you release those outdated identities?

Who have you not forgiven yet?

What boundaries would serve and empower your growth and flourishing?

What undelivered communications are you holding onto?

What resentment or grudges are you still holding onto?

The answers to these prompts may reveal a lot to you about where you still have room to heal and grow. If these prompts bring up sadness, anger, anxiety, and other strong emotions, that's okay. That is healthy. You may even consider it a good sign. These feelings must come up, so they can come out. We must surface them to consciously release them. I acknowledge you for taking on the work. This is the beginning of a healing journey that will lead to your financial freedom because something important to understand is that if you accumulate wealth and riches out of resentment, you will be disappointed when you find yourself poor in spirit. It is healing your heart that will make you feel fulfilled in a way that you can truly enjoy your good fortune. I am not selling get rich-quick schemes. I am teaching you how to end generational trauma and poverty.

I want you to know you can go through hard times and come out on the other side. You can go through abusive situations and go on to create multimillion dollar companies, healthy marriages, and happy families. You can face illness, death, disaster, and debt and still rise above. You get to have a life that you love beyond life's challenges. You get to choose it for you.

Repeat after me, *I am worthy of love and abundance and I'm going to go after the life that I desire. I'm going to create the life that I've always dreamed of.*

I have had to tell the fighter in me to put her fists down. Her fight is over.

Something you might not know about Mother Theresa was that she never joined any efforts that were fighting against something. The 'fight' against poverty. 'Fighting' to end hunger and so on. When you hear that people are activists, it conjures images of protesting and marching in the streets wielding signs. Fighting against things is tiresome. It's an exhausting pursuit.

I can attest from my life-long fight that it is physically and emotionally exhausting. The best thing you can do is remove yourself from the fighting situation and promote peace. That is why those journaling prompts will be of such value to you. You will give your heart, mind, and body to release the fight and clear the gunk lodged in your body for all these years. It will free you up to find your inner peace.

Mother Theresa only joined efforts that were pro-peace, pro-abundance, and pro-love. That's how I have decided to be: pro-peace, pro-building dreams, and pro-progress. Instead of staying in a situation to fight against it, I walked away to pursue a more peaceful path, even if that left a few people behind. Someday, my children will learn why they don't see their grandparents, but I will still do my best to promote love when I share that information. I do not hate my parents; I simply will not fight anymore. I welcome love in my life and excuse anything unlike it.

My hope for you in your process of looking into your past is that you bless and release anything that is ready to go. I hope that you are able to make fresh space in your head and heart to welcome in the new blessings that await you. You are worthy of love, peace, and abundance in your life, and I am here to walk with you in this journey. I am glad we are here together.

Chapter 9

Us Vs the World

"If you can dream it, of course you can achieve it.
Write it, speak it, step into it, and it will be yours."

It was February 2010 and Noah and I were heading out on a road trip to Florida for a spring break vacation. It was our first big road trip and vacation together. We were about nine months into our new relationship but truthfully, it wasn't longer than two months into dating that I knew he was the one. We were also about four months into winter in the Midwest and Florida sounded like a perfect destination for the snowiest time of a Wisconsin winter.

So, we started out on our trek. Noah was driving my sporty little white Pontiac and I rode along as a passenger. A sexy man driving my sexy car, I was in heaven. We still had hours to go but the sun was already shining in my world.

On our drive down, we did what every new couple does on their first road trip, read books out loud. Ha! Just kidding, I'm sure most couples don't do that. However, that's what we did. Knowing that we'd have a lot of windshield time, I bought a stack of new books to read out loud while we were driving. The books I brought along were all on the topic of real estate investing and financial freedom, a topic we were both eager to learn about.

In order, I read *Retire Young Retire Rich*, then the *Cashflow Quadrant* and *Rich Dad Poor Dad*, all by real estate mogul Robert Kiyosaki. I could hardly believe my own ears as I was reading this out loud. I started reading about financial freedom, cashflow, and the difference between an employee and an investor. I was shocked at what I was learning about how being an investor, especially a real estate investor, was the way to the freedom I so deeply desired.

All over again, I felt jaded by society and the educational system for not teaching me these things earlier. Here I was, newly graduated with a master's degree and I knew none of this information. Just like when I found out my girlfriend in sales was raking in the dough, I felt like this information was withheld in school. I felt so misguided and that the only way to succeed was through self-education.

Reading these three books on our trip changed it all for me, for us. Noah was just as eager to advance in the real estate business, which he had just started exploring. I loved our kindred spirits, ambitious to take the industry by storm. I was just starting to tap into my entrepreneurial potential, but Noah was a seasoned veteran.

Noah became a successful entrepreneur as a sophomore in high school. At the age of fifteen, he started his own landscaping business. We all know a kid in town who cut lawns, but this was different. This young man had a full-blown business before he had a license to drive. He would have his mom drop him off at clients' houses before school to fit in a few jobs and get right back to work as soon as school was out for the day. He worked day in and day out all summer long from the moment the weather broke in the spring until winter hit; or until hunting season, if we're being honest.

I was twenty-five when I met him, at the age of twenty-one, and he was well into his successful career as a landscaper. We met just as he was making his first attempts at entering the real estate world and I was thrilled to take this adventure together. But first was our adventure to Florida. I read and rode along as Noah drove, only stopping for gas and the most amazing smoothies in the entire world at *Robert is Here Fruit Stand* in Homestead, Florida. We still need to go back for those smoothies. Pulling up to that ocean full of aqua-blue water was one of the most amazing views I'd ever seen.

We had a great time on our trip continuing the conversations about business ownership and success. Like I mentioned early on, within two short months of dating, I knew he was the one. We both knew. What an exciting and exhilarating moment it was to feel that together. Even though we knew this, we still took the time to get to know each other better and validate those initial butterfly feelings and this trip together was confirming it for us. We have always been great partners and truly enjoy each other. Our relationship has only developed and matured over the years.

From very early on, we would dream up a vision about farming and having a family. While getting to know each other, we discovered that we had so much in common with our farm backgrounds, 4-H, FFA, raising animals, working on farms, working hard, and physical labor. Both Wisconsin born and raised, we just get each other. We have the same values and visions and that works well for us.

We were thrilled to find out that we both had an equal love for hunting and the outdoors. In fact, he didn't know how much hunting meant to me until our first deer hunting season together. On opening day, he left early without me and said he would come back and get me. He came back in the afternoon only to find me in tears because I hardly ever missed an opening morning of deer season. When he picked me up, he took me to his grandma's land, and I shot a small doe within an hour. He realized right then and there that I was the one for him. Hunting means a lot to him, and it means a lot to me. To find someone so compatible felt like magic and we both knew it. Needless to say, he's never underestimated my love of hunting ever again.

It especially seems like magic when I think about how we met. If we're being serious here, I really do believe that I actually manifested Noah into my life. Well, when I tell you the full story, you might be able to tell that we manifested each other. I shared what a master manifestor is in an earlier chapter, and your manifestation lesson starts now.

Back then, I vividly remember being so heartbroken and sad that I hadn't found my dream guy yet. I surely thought I would've been married already instead of partying every weekend. I remember feeling sorry for myself and my friends telling me, "You can't just expect to find the man of your dreams to show up in your front yard! If you want to meet your dream husband, you must put yourself out there and go mingle. You must go meet people, be social, etc." So, I did, I was going out and trying to be social, but I was still feeling pretty hopeless.

I'm not sure how the inspiration came about but eventually, I decided to make a list of exactly what I was looking for in my dream husband. I began to visualize the perfect man coming into my life. I prayed for him. I knew he was there. I believed he was out there. I hoped that someday, some way, somewhere, I would find him. From my rented basement apartment, I would look out the window and pray every night and read my list of my dream man.

I had just moved into this basement apartment around January and was doing this practice for a couple months when I remember being woken up by loud machines outside my window on a dewy March morning. At the time, I worked for a non-profit agricultural organization where I attended evening meetings. I sometimes didn't get home until midnight or later. This happened to be one of those mornings when I slept in after a late night. Hearing all the commotion, I peeked out my window and saw a cute, younger guy on a tractor working on installing the new seeding for the lawn.

My jaw dropped. *Could* the man of my dreams show up in my front yard?!? I had certainly been reading that list while staring out of the very same window I was now staring at what seemed to be a cute man on a tractor. I couldn't see much of his face since his hood was up and he was wearing a ball cap. He also didn't talk much but I could tell he was somewhere around my age. *Could* he have really rolled into my life on a tractor?!?

I was remembering everyone telling me to put myself out there; that if I wanted to meet the man of my dreams, I wasn't going to meet him by hiding in my basement. So, I got up, got ready, made myself presentable, and went outside. There he was, standing in my front yard, and I was standing on the doorstep. I didn't know it then, but I went outside to say "Hi" to the rest of my life.

He was wearing all his finest attire, a green ragged sweatshirt with the hood up, baseball cap, jeans, and boots. I was already smitten. However, Johnny, the sixty-something-year-old guy that was helping him at the time made a joke that I was the homeowner's girlfriend. I made sure to make it abundantly clear that I was the tenant renting the lower level and that I was *single.* I also mentioned that I wasn't planning to rent forever and that I was looking to buy a farm in the country because I grew up on a farm and had a horse boarded outside of town.

I wanted to make sure that if this cute guy, who was barely talking, was at all interested in me, he knew what kind of person I was and what I was looking for in life. I wanted to make sure that if this was my only shot to make an impression, that he could get to know me a little bit. Clearly it worked because a few weeks later, my landlord, Andy, said they were talking about me and that we have a lot in common.

Remember how I said Noah manifested me as well? Have you ever heard the phrase, *if you build it, they will come?* Turns out, he had a part in helping build the house that I rented the basement of. I don't know if he ever had a list of his dream woman anywhere, but he built a house and then I showed up in it. Then here I go, wishing upon a star out of the house he built and poof, he shows up laying seed in the front yard. The surprise of our lives, for sure.

Andy gave me Noah's number, but I was still a bit too nervous to reach out. Then one night, I had some friends over for drinks and they convinced me to call him. Nothing like a little liquid courage to help take the leap. He didn't answer but I had enough beers in me not to sweat it. He officially had my number and the conversations via text started. For a couple weeks, we just texted back and forth, learning little bits and pieces about each other.

Finally, for my birthday in early June, I invited Noah to join us at the local one horse, Wisconsin-style watering hole that had a glass-front cooler with cheese for sale at the back of the bar. I was still in my party stage of life and was sure to be the life of the party. In true Wisconsin fashion, instead of ordering a round of drinks for every-one at the bar, I ordered a block of cheese and started cutting it and handing out slices to everyone. I could tell I was really starting to win over the love of my life with my Midwest generosity.

The night got really wild really quickly when I reached my limit of drinks and was operating off of liquid courage again. I ordered a pizza and ran out of the door without paying because I knew the bartender and thought I was being funny. Noah was not laughing but played along anyway. Here he was, an upstanding citizen, and honest man, entertaining a drunk crush on her wild birthday week-end. There are a few incidents in our relationship that I can only look back on and laugh and thank God he stuck around to find out more, because the jokester I was hopped into his truck for the first time with a stolen pizza and what was left of an also stolen block of cheese. It was a classy move. Being from rural Wisconsin, we were in a small town, and it was all in good fun, but I am really grateful that wasn't my first and last impression.

I had a sober chance at a second impression shortly after on our first 'real' date at Buffalo Wild Wings. We compared stories about our background, our dreams for the future, and more. Something on our date caught me by complete surprise; I had never met anyone who talked more than I did. He barely talked when I met him on my lawn. I did a lot of talking and shouting and dancing at the bar on my birthday weekend so when, for the first time, I found a guy that could outtalk me, I was impressed and intrigued to say the least.

Love was in the air that summer and it was summer love at its finest. We had just officially started dating. I would go for my after-noon runs around town and he would drive by and wave between landscaping jobs. We worked together in my garden, and I helped with landscaping projects. He would make time to take me fishing at a private pond that had a raft. We would jump off it into the crisp, blue water, and swim around, falling more in love by the minute. We talked and talked and learned about each other's goals and dreams.

I was intrigued by his charismatic personality and his gleeful entrepreneurial spirit. He knew he would be successful. There was no question in his mind and there was really no question in my mind, either. It was just a matter of time. Noah is a true entrepreneur and to this day he has never known what it is like to be an employee. He has never submitted a resume to anyone. He didn't have a college degree or health insurance and wasn't contributing to a 401K when I met him. He didn't even have so much as an email address, but these conventional measurements of success meant nothing about his worth or capabilities. He was a success all on his own and knew he was destined to reach great heights, with or without taking a traditional route.

Fun fact about Noah is that he has been diagnosed as dyslexic for as long as he can remember. Now calling this his super-power, when he was younger, it certainly didn't feel that way. He didn't like being called on to read aloud and he worked with tutors several nights per week to learn how to read. He always felt like school was a waste of time, especially as he got older, and he realized that school was a waste of the prime time of the day for landscaping. He used to sit by the window so he could daydream about being outside. Despite all his challenges in school, he calls dyslexia his super-power largely because it forged a path for him to break the mold.

His brain has been wired to see things differently than most. He has always known that he was smarter than anyone gave him credit for, and he just wanted to get out of school so he could start a business and go do something, create something, and make things happen. Math became his strong suit, and it doesn't take him long to figure out whether a deal is a good financial decision or not. He is sharp, talented, and wise. His smarts have taken him so far, so quickly, and there is no limit to what he can achieve. His clarity and determination are just two of the many things I love about him.

That clarity and determination gives him quite a bit of confidence as well; enough to qualify him as a bit of a rebel. Well, a leader really, but when you use your leadership to go against the grain, 'rebel' becomes the label. Noah staged school petitions and walk-outs when his favorite shop teacher's contract was unfairly non-renewed for the following year. Noah took it upon himself to rally most of the student body together and stage a school walk-out. That stunt ended in him and roughly ten of his friends in court for truancy, which the judge threw out immediately.

Just because he knew who he was, didn't mean everyone recognized his potential. During class, his high school English teacher tried to make a point that if students didn't go to college, they weren't going to go far in the world. This was such a common message in school, but Noah of course saw past it. He was making the same amount of money as his teachers during his final years of high school, and he mostly only worked during the summer months.

"College would be a waste of time for me. Besides, all I need to learn is how to sign the back of a check," Noah fired back swiftly at the teacher who said college was the only way to be successful.

This obviously caused a bit of tension, but it didn't matter for Noah. He saw through the 'school is everything' narrative, but of course, it took him years to learn how to believe in himself, and he certainly has the right to. He went through the pressure of becoming a better reader and student but in the end, marched to the beat of his own drum and has reached financial freedom before a lot of those teachers who doubted or judged him. In fact, that teacher who told him he wouldn't amount to anything if he didn't go to college is the very same teacher who called us looking for a place to rent years later.

It is natural that many parents are afraid when they find out their child has been diagnosed with dyslexia or any disability. They might fear for their futures and the limitations they will face or must overcome. They fear that they won't be able to make it into college and society has made it seem that without college you will not make it in life. We all have different skill sets and potential. When we focus on the assets, instead of the deficiencies, we can see the potential. Focusing on the potential is a skill Noah and I found in each other.

We both set our sights on the potential of financial freedom. We both have a healthy love of and appreciation for money and we set out to climb the ladder of success together. That was made even more clear on our first road trip. We left Florida with sunburns and an excitement to get back to Wisconsin and start on this exciting new journey together. We had such good conversations during that entire trip. It was so refreshing to have found someone who was just as eager for this information as I was, and equally as transformed in this area.

From that road trip, and a lot more research, I was hooked. I was ready. I was eager to learn as much as I could and soak it all in. I wanted freedom. I wanted to live life on our terms. I could see that the income I was making then wasn't going to get me the dream life I had always wanted and so I set out to learn as much as I could to launch a successful real estate business together.

The summer we spent falling in love, we talked about his landscaping business and how to grow it. While he was gone on a fishing trip in Canada, I took it upon myself to get him a logo, a website, and an email account; his first email account. True progress, folks. I also got him set up with a Facebook page and search engine optimization services so more people could find him because as you can assume, he had no internet presence. Honestly, he still doesn't. Anything you see online for Noah is run by yours truly.

Noah's best method of marketing is still by word of mouth. Yet, he was very willing to let me support him any way I could, and I was excited to, so we took a closer look at the development of his biz that would bring in more cash flow. To expand his services, he bought a truck and snowplow attachment to allow for working in the winter when he wasn't landscaping. This worked well but we had our sights set higher.

As we were thinking of other jobs for him to do in the wintertime, the idea of fixing and selling homes came up. He already had some experience in helping with the house I had moved into and a few others but was ready to take it to the next level. This was definitely new territory for me. I didn't know anything about 'fix and flips' but that didn't mean I wasn't willing to learn. I had seen 'house flipping' shows on HGTV. They weren't as prevalent when we started but they became more popular as we got going. It seemed like we had entered at the front of a wave.

Of course, I love the potential of more money, but I want to share something personal with you as well. My whole goal with investing in real estate wasn't necessarily like, *oh my God I can't wait to be a landlord,* but when I met my husband, he was the main breadwinner by a long shot. Even though I was the one with a bachelor's and master's degree, my income could not possibly support the life and family we were planning.

I'm not even kidding when I tell you that man would shimmy up a tree using his pinky finger, chainsaw in tow, to trim the skinny branches. I would be standing on the ground covering my eyes and holding my breath so I didn't have to witness what could potentially happen.

He'd be swinging around in the tree teasing me because he knew what a nervous wreck it made me. "I'm fine, honey! I've got this!" he'd yell as he revved the chainsaw like a wild man.

I would be cringing at the tree trunk thinking, "This is not okay! My heart can't take this!"

I decided right then and there that we needed a back-up plan for the future of our family's income. I needed to protect us against the 4 D's: death, divorce, disaster, and disability. The way Noah was climbing trees, he was putting us at risk of all four. We are all at risk of the 4 D's and after watching my brave…maybe reckless…guy risk his life for a bush, I knew we needed the assurance of income that was disaster-proof.

My definition of financial freedom is "making money, no matter what happens." It is having the kind of financial awareness, education, and structures that will protect you from all the threats that could potentially happen. I wanted to be protected against the 4 D's and the more I learned about real estate, the more I knew it could provide that safety. When I had read those books on our road trip, watched videos, and learned that real estate investing is one of the best, fastest, most efficient ways to build unshakable wealth, I was willing to dive in full force…even if that turned me into a landlord.

I cannot say with all honesty that I had lifelong dreams of being a real estate investor, but as you know my story well by now, you might see that real estate chose me. From my cousin rolling down the drive in Cadillacs to the man of my dreams opening my world to exponential opportunity, it seemed like an obvious choice to make. At first, I thought real estate, owning land, and being a landlord would be daunting, but the more I studied and the more steps we took, it all worked and panned out. Real estate made sense to me and as I have grown our business, it makes more sense to me every day.

As I begin to teach you more about financial freedom, I will share more about real estate too. This book is meant to offer you financial freedom, no matter what vehicle you choose to drive on your way to your dream life. Real estate just happens to be my favorite, but I will keep the conversation diverse for you and you can swap out my examples with the route you are taking, and it will be just as applicable. In fact, at the bottom of this chapter, I will teach you how to become a master manifestor, but you don't have to manifest your dream husband like I did.

As we wrap up this chapter, the beginning of our love story, I want to take a special moment to acknowledge the amazing man that I did end up manifesting. For the man who hardly spoke two words out on that lawn, he opened up his heart once we got to know each other. I met him in a ragged sweatshirt and baseball cap. He may not have had a college degree, but you know what he did have? Charm. He sang songs into my voicemails in those first stages of dating. He still charms me with his sweet smile and tender love.

I wrote that list and then found him, my Noah. The most amazing life and business partner, and one of God's gifts to humanity. He is generous, kind, thoughtful, and reliable for me and the thousands we serve. My husband is my angel and my foundation when I want to crumble. He is the strong and steady arms holding me tight when I'm a mess. I am so blessed to call him my husband and the daddy of our two beautiful children. He is my rock. He is my everything. Thank you, Noah, for being all of who you are. I love you as much as the summer we fell in love.

Okay okay, I had to put that there. Partially because it is so true. I love that man more than anything and partially because we are heading into the hot mess, we made in the real estate world. It's fun, I promise, but it was a mess, too. I am about to take you through a journey of what not to do as you venture into financial freedom. But first, let's talk about your manifestation skills.

⊗ Master Manifestor Bonus

One of the fastest ways to manifest what you want is to know what you want.

For funsies, I've tried years later to find that original list of my dream man but it is lost somewhere. Here is what I remember of it:

1. A man I could have a business with, where we got to work together and not have to be apart during the day, only to see each other at night. I wanted to be able to be a team and work in our business together. I wanted to work with my husband as a husband-wife team.
2. Tall, dark, and handsome. I loved brown eyes and brown hair.
3. Stronger than me. I was a strong girl and I'm still strong. I wanted a man with muscles who was physically stronger than me.
4. Being a rural Midwesterner, he must love the outdoors, hunting, fishing, farming, cows, animals.
5. Being loving, kind, and compassionate.
6. He must love to travel with me and be interested in getting away to see new things.
7. Always be there for me. Make me laugh. Make me feel loved.

Now it's your turn to write a list of dreams you have.

Think of details of the type of person you want to call into your life, the kind of friends, the details of a home you'd like to have, etc. The more specific, the better.

Start writing these down and make your list!

The secret sauce to manifestation is aligned action. When I made this list and knew what I wanted, I was able to recognize it when Noah walked into my front yard and further confirm it as we got to know each other, but I had to take the aligned action of walking outside and making myself available. I sent the text, I made the invitation, I stole the cheese, and then I stole his heart.

Everything you want in life is on the other side of clarity and determination. Noah and I have both and we have a lot of what we desire in life with plenty more on the way. Sure, I manifested a man, but this same exercise can be done for anything you can dream up. You can be a master manifestor, too, if you are willing to realize exactly how powerful you are. If you can dream it, of course you can achieve it. Write it, speak it, step into it, and it will be yours.

Chapter 10

School of Hard Knocks

*"If you are truly ready to enter the journey toward financial freedom,
you are going to encounter more adversity. Nobody who enters gets
a free pass. Nobody. These are the moments to find out what you're
made of and to find out how far you're willing to go,
and if you keep reading, you'll go far."*

I wasn't always a perfect manifestor. There is an age-old adage that says *you'll always find what you are looking for,* and you will. Too often though, you are not consciously clear about what you are looking for.

For example, growing up, my parents would blame so many things on 'Murphy's Law,' which is an epigram that states anything that can go wrong, will go wrong. They would often reference it in a joking manner but in the long run, there was nothing funny about it. We frequently used Murphy's Law as the reasoning and justification for any of our mishaps, misfortunes, challenges, and disappointments. I heard it constantly and learned to use it myself as a means of coping with things not going my way.

I spent most of my younger years following along with this 'joke' that if anything can go wrong, it will…and believe me, it did! I was always fearing for the worst and so that was what I was manifesting for a long time. Mishap after mishap. One bad break after another. There were a handful of years that I fell into a deep depression because I wasn't sure of my worth, since I couldn't seem to string together more than a few good days. It was a real struggle to feel like a good person who bad things just kept happening to.

You see, when you set out on the journey toward financial freedom, you inadvertently bring your past with you. You don't mean to, but you don't know you are doing it. You don't know because until you wake up to the way your past has shaped you, it is you. You are it. There is no separation so you cannot make a change to what you cannot recognize is holding you back.

What you have been through affects what you will go through next, cause and effect. This can be a positive or negative, but the rule stands all the same. If you set your sights on a full life, you will eventually have to decide what parts of your past get to be healed and released and which lessons and attributes will come with you into your future. You can thank the past for the lessons it has taught you but to bring it with you is just dragging around your emotional baggage. It gives you an unfair disadvantage to try to climb the mountains of your goals with backpacks full of bricks. You have the freedom to forge onward with the lessons but not the negative effects of those lessons.

Before I understood this concept, Murphy's Law was apparent in every area of my life. I developed a jaded personality. I carried this jadedness around with me for a few decades and it cost me so much time, money, and energy. I didn't just believe the worst would happen; I *trusted* the worst would happen.

When I was pregnant with my daughter, I was afraid of getting preeclampsia like my mother did with all four of her children. I kept telling everyone a due date for Tesla that was a month earlier than the due date the doctors had given me. I manifested getting preeclampsia and had my daughter at thirty-four weeks, just like I believed, because I am a powerful manifestor. I just started out as a sloppy one.

Well, I can give myself more credit than 'sloppy' because I didn't know better then. Just as I described a few paragraphs back. We cannot transform what we don't know is holding us back. I had no idea that my limiting beliefs were limiting my life, really. I did not understand that. So, I put myself through my very own curriculum in the school of hard knocks. Life was the teacher, but I was taking a self-prescribed crash course.

One of my most learned lessons from the school of hard knocks: be careful what you wish for. We don't always 'wish' badly for ourselves but when we believe in the worst happening, the universe responds in kind. It says your wish is my command and we accidentally command the worst by constantly fearing and ruminating on it.

One of my strongest traits is being stubborn. Part of being stubborn is needing to be right. Part of needing to be right is refusing to be wrong. When you refuse to be wrong, you are unavailable to learn. This proved to be a very difficult strategy for learning anything without an ass-kicking lesson in the process.

In life, this made things challenging. In family, this caused fights and brawls. In career, this caused exhaustion. In motherhood, this caused confusion. In marriage, this caused arguments and cold shoulders. Almost all the time, it cost me more of my precious time, money, and energy than it was worth. This really peaked when we were successful in business, but I had not yet begun to clear the limiting beliefs of my past.

We had reached a point in which we were flourishing with our homebuilding company, but I would take criticism extremely personally. I couldn't handle it when a customer was upset. It would send me in a tailspin of crying in the bathroom at our office. I adopted the belief that people were jerks to cope with and justify my feelings. Murphy's Law, right?

It wasn't long before I began manifesting these sorts of worst-case circumstances in my life and business. I became afraid of my own customers and was struggling with crippling fear that they would end up disappointed. Low and behold, that is exactly what started showing up in our business. The work we loved and enjoyed became a job, a burden, and a huge drag.

I had lost and forgotten the happy-go-lucky person I was before.

I had forgotten how much I loved people. I had forgotten how much fun I had bringing people together and in turn, had forgotten how to be myself. I became a bitter, angry, resentful person that I didn't know anymore, but I still didn't know how to change that. It took quite a bit more manifesting my own misery before I decided to make a change.

One of the most reliable ways of manifesting my own misery was reminding myself how broken I was. When we have limiting beliefs that we haven't identified, we identify *as* them. All of my limiting beliefs about money or hardships weren't limiting beliefs at the time. I *was* limited. I *was* broken.

It was during my year of depression in 2014, when I was so broken inside and broke financially, that without trying to be funny, I showed up to my thirtieth birthday dinner on a bike affectionately named 'Trusty Rusty.' I dug it out of the garage of one of our rental houses where we had finally just evicted tenants who were eleven months late on rent. You read that right, one, two, three, four, five, six, seven, eight, nine, ten, and yes, eleven months late on their rent… because broke landlords have broke tenants. That's how it goes when you truly identify with your limiting beliefs. You don't have them, you *are* them.

So here I was, turning thirty on Trusty Rusty with a real wrench in the spokes of my life. I had a lot of time to think about my sad situation as I pedaled the eighteen miles to my birthday 'celebration.' In my twenties, I had a very different vision for how far I'd be by age thirty and my visions didn't include being broke as hell, riding a rickety bike down the highway to a nice restaurant for my birthday dinner. I only went out of my way because I knew they were going to pay for my meal. Otherwise, I would have rather crawled under a rock and hid for the rest of ever. I felt like a complete loser.

However, you could say this was my entry ticket into the world of entrepreneurialism. Basically, a let's-see-what-she's-made-of kind of entry ticket. At this stage of the game, we were already considered real estate investors. Well, maybe by definition, but we certainly hadn't made it by any means. We had made $90k on our fix and flip homes but were still playing very risky investing games. We were still learning how to be true leaders, and landlords who charged rent. I was, in fact, investing in real estate, but I was a total mess and felt less trusty than old Rusty.

This wouldn't be the only time I had to charge forth past my pride and past my mistakes. You met me in the preface of this book, sitting in the valley of one of my deepest letdowns; our $150,000 subdivision loss mid 2015. At thirty, I was trying to gain any little ounce of success and momentum in our lives. We were married, trying to build businesses that would sustain our futures, and I was feeling so ready to start a family.

Although we were finally gaining traction in our business leading up to the subdivision saga, we had been holding out on having children until we could get our feet under us financially. We were finally seeing success after the years of scraping by but that hard of a setback was causing my dreams to crumble right before my eyes. This was not an oopsie kind of mistake where you just shrug your shoulders and walk away from a failed attempt. We were on the hook for a lot of money that put us behind on a lot of personal and professional deadlines.

I didn't want to wait much longer to have kids but there was no way I wanted to bring children into the world when we were flirting with the financial edge so much. I couldn't have a newborn when we were ready to sell our home and live in a cardboard box. We were already stretching ourselves so thin to make our dreams come true and this hit took every last breath of wind right out of my sails. This is why I say that all the money in the world can't fulfill or fix your mindset. Your beliefs will always outweigh your earnings. My broken mentality had manifested in full form at this point.

Only in retrospect can I say we were some of the most dedicated entrepreneurs out there but it didn't feel that triumphant in the most challenging moments. We really risked it all for our dreams but some of those days put my psyche to the test. Building our dreams felt glamorous to say, but building our business took clarity, dedication, work, and emotional endurance that we didn't necessarily have.

Noah's landscaping business was the only thing sustaining us at the time while we tried our hand at real estate and construction. Our first attempt at a larger project than fix-and-flips failed. I felt like a failure. I was scared about the debt we had just accrued. Even though I was married to the man of my dreams, and I was grateful for that, I was scared for our future. We were hanging out on the edge, clawing, scrapping, yearning for success of our own.

The one thing that kept me tethered to reality during the challenging growth years were the workout classes I was going to. Right around the time I quit my job in 2013, I joined a gym and started attending 5:30am workout classes in my hometown. I dare say, those classes kept me alive during such a dark time in life. Those classes were a way to workout and meet people from my community. I hadn't been part of my local community much because my previous job had demanded that I travel to six counties regularly, and I had only been associating with my coworkers. All of that ended with my job, and suddenly, I felt very lonely.

After class, I didn't want to go home because I knew what the rest of the day would be like. I would get home to silence. Noah would have already left for work. I would count on him being gone, though, because the days I would get home before he left were hard for me. He would leave the house as his cheerful self just like one of Snow White's jolly dwarfs marching toward the door singing, "Hi-ho-hi-ho, it's off to work I go!"

I would scowl at him. I was jealous of his cheerfulness; his zest for life; his confidence in himself. He was busy all day, hustling from one job to the next, and here I was, clueless about what to do. We would have a predictable exchange where he would ask me what was wrong and I would respond with that infamous "nothing…" which really means "everything! Please pull it out of me."

I would cry and tell him, "I don't know what to do. I don't know how to be an entrepreneur. What do I do?"

Like an optimistic mentor from a movie scene he would gleefully respond, "You can do anything! Just think of something and do it! That's the beauty of being an entrepreneur!" while I still stood there, holding my hands out, looking for a more legitimate answer. I wanted a clear direction or instruction. Then he'd shrug and head out the door because he was going to be late for his successful entrepreneurial venture.

It only took a few of those exchanges to realize that I didn't know how to not be told what to do. I didn't know how to make up my own agenda. I didn't know how to be this free. I really was the rule follower I was brought up to be and this only brought on more sadness at the time. I remembered that I used to be as energized as my husband was now, prior to this huge life transition.

Now, I was scared and alone, and I couldn't relate to my friends anymore. I was trying my hand at real estate and getting a miserably slow start. I was tired, scared, and again, totally broke. I could now afford less than when I was teaching and felt lower than ever. Friends and family would ask me why I wouldn't just 'get a job,' but I was determined to figure out this new life. I was determined to make it on my own. I was determined that entrepreneurship was for me and I wasn't going to go down this easy. I quickly learned that getting your ass handed to you was the price of admission in order to survive entrepreneurship and live a life of freedom. I felt like I had gone from high school to college in the school of hard knocks.

Soon enough, our relationship started to suffer because I hated everything. I couldn't buy my own clothes. I had to stretch every grocery trip as far as we could. I didn't have a car and to make matters worse, I accidentally filled his new snow plowing truck up with unleaded fuel and it was a diesel truck, almost ruining the engine. I hated our house. I hated everything. I was bitter, angry, and resentful of his cheerfulness. I was spiraling quickly.

I would then try to research business ideas without knowing what I was doing. I didn't know what to do with all the time I had. Even though we had flip projects, I still felt confused about my role in it all. I felt aimless and angry. I would read self-help inspirational books to try to boost me up, but I just spent a lot of time crying and ended up going into a deep, dark hole.

The morning that everything changed, I sat on the floor crying next to my bed. The sadness was coming from the depth of me. It was such a deep, soul level pain. I remember the dark hole. I saw the darkness. I heard voices telling me, 'Look at you, you have a bachelor's degree. You have a master's degree. You are nearly thirty years old and haven't made anything of yourself yet. You gave up a job you loved. You were on the top of your game. You gave that up for this? What a loser. You are worthless."

I wailed out loud because I believed those words. I could hardly stand myself. I couldn't, really. Thoughts of suicide came flooding in with the voice saying, 'You could just end it now and not have to figure this out anymore. Life is too hard and too heartbreaking. You could just be done.' That was when I knew I had met the devil. That was when I knew I was as low as I would get. I had reached the bottom. The ache in my heart was too much to bear.

As I mentioned in the preface, the second I recognized the devil, I remembered that I knew God and I had a flash-like awakening. One moment I was listening to those voices and the next moment, I stopped. It suddenly dawned on me that the only person that was going to pull me through this was me. Yes, I was surrounded by the presence of God, but I would have to be the one to climb out of this hole and start living my life differently. No one else could get me out of this. Noah did everything he could, and I resented him. It had to be me, so I let it be. I chose life. I chose myself. I chose my future, and I chose entrepreneurship all over again.

To kick off this new stage, I planned a trip to Hawaii, solely funded by credit cards. I didn't tell Noah that detail because I knew he would refuse, but I knew it was what I needed at that time. It was July and I planned the trip for December of that year to end the most brutal year of my life. It also gave me something to look forward to as I worked my way out of that hole.

When the trip came, we hiked, swam in waterfalls, ate fresh sushi and ahi tuna steaks, sipped our early morning coffee with bagels and lived it up. It was awesome. That trip reset me and my focus. It was very restorative for me. My attitude started to shift and improve, and our relationship started healing as a result. It was a turning point that altered the trajectory of our future. That was our life-saving trip.

This can be a life-saving book for you if you lean all the way into its message. I would like to invite you to take a moment to consider the school of hard knocks you might have put yourself through. I ask you to consider the limiting beliefs that you have. You may not see them straight away because you cannot call them beliefs when they seem like facts.

Just because we have believed something our whole lives doesn't make it true, but I want to reinforce the hope that things can change for you. What might seem helpless or hopeless can be worked out for the best. Life can get better. Your circumstances can improve, but I will tell you, you will be the one to improve them.

There is something very important that I will remind you of a few times in this book: trauma is not a competition. I have shared some of my struggles and we have all faced adversity. Adversity, by definition, is an instance of serious misfortune or a state of continued difficulty. In Latin, it literally means, 'turned against' or 'hostile or unfavorable.' Adversity is something to face and overcome and no doubt, you have. You are here reading this book. You have overcome something to get here and that is not to be overlooked.

We have a right to say what has felt hard for us and we don't have a right to diminish or compare someone else's challenges. We all have a journey here that serves an important purpose and our unique setbacks shape us to turn out differently and inspire us to make a difference in unique ways.

I would like to invite you to take a short break from this book to journal about some of the toughest times you've faced in your life. I encourage you to take your time in this journaling opportunity because as I have made as clear as possible in this chapter, unless we mindfully heal and clear our past, we will drag it into our future.

 # Overcoming Challenges

What were times of difficulty in your life?

What 'bottoms' have you hit?

What heartaches have you faced?

What limiting beliefs do you still identify with?

What are you manifesting that you would rather not be?

What trials and tribulations have you overcome to get this far?

Has there ever been a time where your road has split into two paths and you've had a choice to make on which way you would go?

Now think/write about what you did to overcome your hardships.

What got you through the hard times?

Who got you through the challenges?

What supports you the most when you are facing hard times?

What help do you know you need when you are struggling in life?

How can you be sure to get your needs met when you know you need help?

Overcoming the odds, difficulties, or challenges make us stronger as we surpass them, one by one. They make our life story much more interesting, at the very least. You have been through hardship. It is imperative to acknowledge what you have already overcome so that you may continue to forge ahead. You have been through your own school of hard knocks. Heck, maybe you are in the thick of it right now…but don't give up.

It is time to turn your pain into your purpose and use your adversities as fuel to start your adventures. If you are truly ready to enter the journey toward financial freedom, you are going to encounter more adversity. Nobody who enters gets a free pass. Nobody. These are the moments to find out what you're made of and to find out how far you're willing to go, and if you keep reading, you will go far.

Chapter 11

Trial By Fire

"Risk comes with the territory of playing for great reward."

Say it with me: I love money.

For us to continue this journey, I am going to make it abundantly clear; I love money. I love to love money. Money loves me. I love earning it, receiving it, saving it, and spending it. Good lord, do I love spending it. You know why? Because I know and trust that my spending…my investing…will come back to me ten-fold, and it does, because I love money and money loves me. Money loves us.

Noah loves money, too. He loves what money can be used for and all that it makes possible, not just for our family but for this world. I've already told you that I was raised being told that money isn't everything and I want to say that it sure makes everything a lot easier. You may have also heard that money can't buy happiness, but I have never bought into that statement. Money sure can buy happiness. It can fulfill dreams and empower you to take care of yourself in a way that supports your well-being, and yes, your happiness.

I want you to know that it is okay if deep down, you know and believe that money can make a substantial difference in your life. It is okay to want to obtain more of it and we will work on that together, but you must be able to admit, to yourself and others, that you do in fact want to accumulate more of it. Money is one of the most abundant, powerful, and functional tools on this planet. Money talks and money walks. Money moves fluidly, and I am going to teach you to move with it. I am going to teach you to dance to the beat of the money drum because you get to have fun and make a massive difference with money.

A lot of my lessons with money are all about me getting my stubborn ass handed to me in business, and life for that matter, but I want to reiterate that my bold moves are driven by that alluring promise of financial freedom and it has always paid off, in the long run. I share that because I want to make this a safe conversation and exploration for you. You are allowed to love money and you are certainly allowed to go after it.

So again, repeat after me.

I. Love. Money.

Very good, friend. So let's talk about what a mess I have made with money. Well, let's talk about risk, because so often, a big reward requires a big risk and a hell of a lot of courage.

You already know about our biggest loss, the subdivision debacle, but Noah and I have taken lots of risks similar or greater. The $150,000 we lost on the subdivision mattered so much because it was the most money we had ever dealt with at one time. Since that dreary day, we have moved and made millions and although I would never wish for such a situation again, I know we could survive it. That is a major factor in playing big; you learn how to play.

Risk comes with the territory of playing for great reward. Everyone lands somewhere on the scale of being risk averse but some of us can handle more nerve-wracking chances than others. Many, mainly my bookkeeper and lender, would consider me a daredevil when it comes to taking risks, but my mind is centrally focused on the potential; the reward. I am willing to find out. I am someone willing to feel incredibly uncomfortable when making the leap from good to great. I could say it is just in regard to finance, but that is true in every area of my life. I risked jumping between my parents at age five and I am willing to jump off the cliff of courage in family, business, motherhood, and even my health.

As we move on with a conversation about risk, I want to teach you the idea that there are two kinds of risk to manage: tangible and intangible. Tangible means having to do with the senses like taste, touch, see, and smell. Tangible risk comes with tangible consequences. Losing your house, not having a meal, accumulating debt, getting physically hurt or harmed. Tangible risks that have outcomes such as these include taking a gamble. This could mean gambling with your finances or health. It could put others at risk as well.

Intangible risks have an intangible impact. Meaning others cannot *see* it but it is certainly there and has a less measurable effect to the naked eye. This does not mean, however, that its impact is unknown. It just means we cannot touch or taste it. An intangible risk won't cost us our livelihood or put us out on the street.

Let's look at the intangible risk of 'taking a chance' or sharing yourself vulnerably. This entire book, I have been sharing my past in a very exposed way. This can be uncomfortable for me, and potentially for you. I am risking triggering your own traumatic memories. I am risking putting myself up for judgment, ridicule, and rejection. We cannot formally touch ridicule or rejection, but we can sense it. These different risks also have their different rewards.

I broke away from my family, which felt so life altering and risky. I decided to share my story, which felt riskier. I have taken one business jump to another. In motherhood, I have adopted unorthodox parenting styles. I have started healing and health practices that make people's eyebrows move up to the middle of their forehead.

All of these risks have their threats, but they also have their tangible and intangible rewards. This may look like mental, emotional, physical, and spiritual rewards that bring us up as much as they threaten to bring us crashing down. Tangibly, we can double our money. We can get the promotion or relationship. We can lose the weight. All things that are clear, measurable, and obvious.

Intangible rewards can turn out like satisfaction, confidence, pride, and notoriety. Trust is a major intangible reward so many of us gamble on. You make promises and when you fulfill them, you become trustworthy, but you better believe you took the risk of not delivering on your word. I told you I would help you achieve financial freedom through my example. I am taking a risk that what I know will help you transform your financial future. That is a risk I am willing to take, but are you?

We have to take a look together right now to find out where you land on the scale of risk aversion. How willing are you to take risks? I strongly encourage you to spend some time considering this. Really sit and think, what am I willing to do to make my dreams happen? Specifically in reference to the shared risk we are partaking in, am I willing to do what it takes to reach financial freedom?

Assessing Your
Risk Capacity

ASSESS	Very Unwilling		Neutral		Very Willing
How willing am I to get my finances in order?	1	2	3	4	5
How willing am I to clean up my spending?	1	2	3	4	5
How willing am I to budget and make a financial plan?	1	2	3	4	5
How willing am I to give up unnecessary spending?	1	2	3	4	5
How willing am I to practice discipline?	1	2	3	4	5

UNCOVER

If you answered 1 or 2 to any of the above, what is holding you back?

REFLECT

Historically, how has risk-taking gone for you? What memories come up when you think about taking risks? Are these positive or negative?

IDENTIFY

Are you encouraged or discouraged when taking risks? How has risk taking impacted you at the different stages of your life?

GROW

How do you currently feel about taking risks? How do you want this to change in the future?

Be real with me. Be real with yourself. Are you ready? Because risks are part of life. When you start anything new, you are taking a risk. You are taking a step forward into the unknown. It is important to consider these questions because I don't want you to quit when the challenges come up, and they will…because life. Life will challenge and tempt you and if you are unclear about your goals and why you are chasing them, you will get distracted and discouraged faster than you can finish this sentence.

These are important things to consider because although they may seem obvious as answers, if we don't actively think about these things, they can subconsciously hold us back. If we believe that we always fail or risks always go bad, we stop taking chances. I told you about how jaded I became in my late twenties and that really held me up for a while. I did not know how my failures, losses, disappointments, hardships were being triggered when I quit my job to go out on my own in life. Before I could really succeed as an entrepreneur, I had to heal and recreate my relationship with risk-taking.

You too may need to heal from some of your losses and letdowns in life before getting back up on the horse to ride into the sunset of success. Therapy is a very supportive means of healing our past in a way that doesn't impede our future. If there is one thing that will put you on the fast track to healing what you have successfully repressed, it is starting your ventures toward your dreams. Any person truly chasing their dreams will confirm for you that what they have had to overcome is what had previously held them back in life. If you are finding yourself stuck or held back, start with your healing journey and it will propel you forward faster than you can imagine.

Healing is something that came after we had made a lot of money and messes in our business. As Noah and I got into real estate, we took classes and got mentors, who all gave us very clear instructions to succeed, and we did just about everything bass ackwards. That's right, we were told to hire out—we did it ourselves. We were told to hire general contractors and realtors, and we became them instead. We were told to never use banks if we didn't have to, and it was the first thing we did.

Part of my stubbornness is my grit. Noah's got a lot of it, too. This chapter is called trial by fire because we hurled ourselves into the fire of learning what not to do by doing it all, against many of our mentors' advice. We both sort of grew up with something to prove and we thought we had the passion and power to prove everyone wrong, and we did.

We were the youngest couple to be inducted into the Hall of Fame for our real estate investing endeavors and got to meet Robert & Kim Kiyosaki on stage in Las Vegas. We became one of the top homebuilding companies in our area. Our successes were shared in stories in the local schools. We grew our family at the same time as growing our business to prove we could do it all. But, we also ran ourselves absolutely ragged in the process. Before I tell you about our Burnout Anniversary, I am going to share a sweeter success story about us taking the risk of literally signing our lives away to buy our first home together.

Noah and I had just read all the *Rich Dad, Poor Dad* books that we could get our hands on, took our first real estate investing course, and started our first LLC together. We were ready to start our fix and flip adventures. There we were, ready to take on the world, ready to tackle the journey of striving for financial freedom. We marched from one side of the street to the next. First to the CPA office to start an LLC together, then to the other side of the street to the local bank to start a bank account for said LLC. We also needed to apply for some credit cards since neither of us had ever taken out a credit card or a loan worth measuring and therefore had basically zero credit.

There we were at the bank, asking for credit cards, opening bank accounts, and requesting a meeting with the owner of the bank. Quite comical in retrospect; just marching in like we had any inkling of anything we were talking about. Then came time for the meeting because yes, the bank owner agreed to meet with us. Mind you, we were not married at the time. Engaged, but not married.

We sat down in the banker's office to talk about investing in real estate. We didn't have any clue what we were talking about. I was hoping my fiancé did because my strategy was to shake in my boots and stare at the floor while Noah did all the talking. He always did. From day one, I knew I had a talker on my hands who could connect with anyone, and he was certainly connected with the banker while I played my role of Nervous Nellie.

Noah had some experience with fixing and flipping homes, so he felt confident, and I was confident in him. He had also remodeled rental units for a local real estate investor in our town so he could speak the language enough to win over the banker. All I can remember about this meeting was that Noah said we were interested in getting started in real estate investing and we wondered if they by chance had any foreclosures on their books that they were looking to sell. This was in 2010, in the aftermath of the 2008 recession, so foreclosures were cropping up everywhere.

Luckily, the lender said yes. He said the bank had taken back an old house in a town about thirteen miles away that we could look at and see if it was something we were interested in buying with the intention of renovating to sell. We immediately stood up, shook hands, and promptly headed to the property.

When we got to the house to check it out, we had to bushwhack our way into the back door. We barely had enough room to stick our heads in and look at it long enough to get an idea of what we would be getting ourselves into. We were getting ourselves into some real shit. We literally had to tiptoe over cat feces and garbage while holding our breath because of the smell of cat urine. I had my shirt over my nose and a very disgusted look on my face when Noah turned to me with his huge, optimistic smile and said, "Let's do it! We can fix it up and move in!"

"Move in? Are you kidding me?" I choked out from under my shirt collar.

I was still renting that basement apartment at the time and so this would be one way I wouldn't have to pay rent anymore. Apparently cleaning cat urine had more perks than paying rent because I agreed. Well, I said yes to Noah's excitement and my trust in us more than the cat pee. I said yes to my own excitement. We went right back to the bank and said we'd take it, and so began our real estate investing career.

Immediately following, the lender sent us to the other side of the street to the insurance office to take out a one-million-dollar life insurance policy of which the bank would have first dibs on if anything were to happen. We literally bet our life on making this real estate investing business happen which put a whole new meaning to 'signing your life away.'

Shortly after, that same bank sold us our second flip house and our first five rental properties, all in foreclosure with no money down for any of them. When we had our first closing of a flip house, we proudly held up the proceeds check to our banker and had a picture of all three of us taken. We went from shaking in our boots to making a profit in less than a year. This success continued for many years to come, and it all started with taking a risk. We didn't have to put any money down on the houses, we had to put our lives on the line. We bet on ourselves, and we won—and we kept winning.

We got our start, and there was no turning back. We started with those two flip homes in 2010 with about a dozen more to follow. Then in 2015, after I came out of my funk, we started building new construction homes with just two to start and went to twelve homes in 2016. We did another twelve in 2017 and bumped up to sixteen homes in 2018. By that point, we knew we needed employees, so we got a few of those, too. We were growing rapidly and averaged seventeen homes a year in 2019, 2020, and 2021. We were constantly maxing out and peaking year after year.

We took that risk and reaped the rewards, but one risk we all take as dream-chasers is burnout. Even though my husband and I have the best relationship in the entire world, we have faced our challenges in growing an insanely successful business together. We've always held the same vision of growth, but we've also had massive blowups during this journey as well. We're real people in a real relationship and how hard we were working pushed us to many limits. In fact, in our third year of averaging seventeen houses, we had one of the most distinct blowups that became the final straw of total burnout for me. I was ready to throw in the towel of our business to save our marriage and our sanity.

December 4th is what I affectionately refer to as our Burnout Anniversary. It was a day that marked our decision to get out of custom home building and really look at how we were operating and how we would move forward in our business and lives. We had become successful but had also become victims of our own doing. We were strung up by too many tasks, obligations, responsibilities, and needs.

In the face of a global pandemic, employee loss, supply chain delays, and labor shortages, along with babies in diapers, we realized we were in over our heads. Professionally, we were managing a multimillion-dollar homebuilding and real estate investing company, realty brokerage, and property managing fifty units of commercial and residential tenants all at once. Personally, we had a three-year-old and one-year-old, a nanny on vacation, and a water heater out in the middle of December. Oh, and when I say we, I mean I.

Noah did what Noah usually does in the fall and winter. He went ice fishing. Hunting and fishing are his ways of relaxing. He works hard all year to get to enjoy his annual trips and of course, I want him to be happy and enjoy some time off. This perfect storm of circumstances just happened to be the straw that broke the camel's back for the pace we were performing at.

I called our water heater guy, and he was booked out. I knew he was under the same amount of stress we were trying to keep up with the demand of the season. This resulted in me boiling water on our stove to give myself and our kids sponge baths for the week. I was overworked and stressed out when the calls started coming in.

I was at the helm of our business, 'putting out fires' as we called it, answering questions to angry homeowners about why contractors weren't showing up to fix this or that. I was hanging up with homeowners only to call said contractors and instill the fear of God in them if they didn't show up to a client's house. It seemed like a week that everyone needed everything from me, and I was feeling like I had nothing left to give.

Then, I cracked. I got a call from a great client asking me why Noah hadn't been getting back to him. I knew why, but it didn't justify him ignoring a client. We had way too many balls in the air, and they were noticeably dropping one by one. Admittedly, Noah was burning out and checking out, big time.

I was so frustrated because I didn't have the choice to check out like he had. He was off ice fishing, and I was left to pick up all the pieces. In a white-hot rage, I went outside and called him from our driveway. I was so angry; I didn't feel the cold as it chilled my bare neck. He was somewhere in the middle of North Dakota sitting on a frozen lake, hovering over a hole he drilled to catch a big walleye for his dinner that night.

"Why don't you just stay in North Dakota and do what you're good at and just keep ice fishing," I scathed through gritted teeth.

I didn't even give him a chance to really answer the phone. I just went right in on him. "Don't worry, I've got this issue too. I can handle it. This is what women were built for. *Cleanup crew on aisle five!* Pooper scooper of the company, it's fine. I got this. Don't you worry about it. I told our client that they called the right person in our team of two. They called the one that would actually get shit done and get it taken care of, while having a one-year-old on my hip and a cell phone to my ear. No worries." I just kept laying into him and hung up before he could even respond. I didn't want to hear any excuses and he couldn't solve my problems from the lake so I promptly hung up and got to work on putting out those fires and getting shit done…all while really falling apart inside.

That wasn't how I wanted to treat my husband that I loved with all my heart. Those weren't really words I wanted to say, and I most certainly wanted him to come home and help me fix the problem we had in front of us. I was so worked up and upset that I just went into my shoulder-it-all-alone mode. I was done with the hustle. I was done with the stress. I was done. Just done. I was just as burnt out as he was, and I think we both finally crossed the threshold into admitting exactly how tired we were.

When he got off the phone, he promptly called the flower shop and had bouquets sent for both my daughter and me. At first, I scoffed in disgust at his attempt to soften me, but I relaxed when he got home, and we talked about what to do. We hugged. We cried. We apologized to each other. We knew this was a sign to transition away from the level of work we had been doing. We knew it was time to figure out something new. We knew this wasn't going to work for us anymore.

The journey to financial freedom will be different for everyone but overworking is something we all might face. It is one of those risks we take on. One of my goals is to teach you how to avoid the pitfalls, hustle culture, and subsequent burnout I experienced at the peak of our production. I want you to slide into financial freedom in a fun way instead of finding out you've become a millionaire and experiencing the worst burnout of your life at the same time.

Noah and I had very big goals, so we played big until it kicked our asses in a big way. We counted on our youth and stamina in a way that didn't really take our humanity into account. We knew we had the capability and capacity to take on a lot. I mean a whole lot. Once I got older and started working with holistic health practitioners, they let me know how much I was up to was a bit alarming and advised me to slow down.

We had plans to retire early so we did our best to maximize our twenties and thirties to bust our asses and do as much as we could. We didn't want to stretch out our working lives. We wanted to work to the bone early, build up our business, establish our legacy, and enjoy it later. Even when we decided to have kids, we didn't want to let up.

Noah would say, "we don't have time yet," or "we're not at that point yet." We lived sparsely. We lived on the edge. We lived so far outside of our comfort zone that we were afraid to have kids because we didn't want to bring up children while taking such huge risks. The interesting part was that we weren't broke. We had just constantly reinvested our profits back into our business in a way that didn't leave us feeling like we had money in the bank. We were investing more money than I used to make in a year.

We were investing so much money, learning so many lessons, losing money, and making money, that we stayed uncomfortable for years on end. Our motto had been "if you're not living on the edge, you're taking up too much space." We can be intense in our focus but as I have shared, this took us to great heights, but also great depths.

One important thing that we did do in our early years when we were fixing and flipping homes was celebrate our most recent sale by going out to lunch or dinner after the closing. Those first few flips were real victories for us but that faded quickly when we started homebuilding. As we took on more clients and projects, we didn't take the time for that lunch. Instead, we would just pick up a sub sandwich or a salad to go and get back to work. We were so hyperfocused on the success and financial freedom that we sort of struggled with tunnel vision.

We reached a peak of production that we had so much to keep up with that we hardly even had time to go to the closings, so even the victory at the end of the work got lost in the shuffle. We kept asking the title company to set us up to e-sign for our closings but that was never an option. We were so busy that we got annoyed by our success. It started to feel inefficient, cumbersome, and daunting. We had completely lost the celebration aspect. We also lost our time freedom in the process. We were rushing through our lives, practically trying to escape what we had created. We lost the excitement as a result and became slaves to our business. This happens for a lot of entrepreneurs, and we didn't really catch it happening until it was already consuming us.

There comes a time in most people's lives when we find ourselves ungrateful for the things we had previously prayed for. We were at that point, but that still wasn't the tipping point for us. We took on more and more and more to see where our breaking point was. We wanted to see how much we could take on. Most single builders would build half as many homes as we did. Most local builders average between three to ten homes per year, depending on the company size. We were at eighteen to twenty homes per year, and we had our sights set on growing, until we hit our Burnout Anniversary head on.

To top it all off, we decided to start our family and were becoming new parents in the process. By no means did I have simple pregnancies and I didn't take much of a maternity leave. I mean it when I say we were all in, in crazy ways. We were toting our babies to closings and home construction sites all the time.

In our naivety, we didn't think we would need childcare because we were self-employed. We figured we could just take the babies with us. That is a book-worthy lesson to share. We quickly learned that we could not do this business, and take on parenthood, at the pace that we were going. We genuinely thought we could take on the world, but very soon started to feel like we were carrying the world on our shoulders.

We were so busy keeping our noses to the grindstone and convincing ourselves not to let up that we didn't take the time to realize that we were at our breaking point. We had these it's-not-over-until-the-money's-in-the-bank attitudes that kept us hustling ourselves silly. We hadn't taken the time to rise above our business to see the full picture until we hit that wall.

We had reached the point where our bodies and spirits were hurting from the stress. We were learning that when you don't feel good enough to enjoy your success, it's not worth it anymore. We had reached two of our most major goals and barely realized or appreciated them. We had achieved financial freedom and become millionaires and yet, all we wanted was to quit the business that got us there.

When I found out that we were on track to have another record-breaking year come up, I promptly buried myself in our bed out of sheer exhaustion. Faceplanting on my bed is not how I envisioned hearing the words, "you've become a millionaire," while simultaneously experiencing the biggest burnout of our lives. That's not what I want for you, either.

As I just mentioned, if you can't enjoy it, it's not worth it. If it steals your joy and excitement for life, that's not financial freedom; that is financial slavery.

Our financial, business, parenthood, health, and life lessons came at us head on because that was how we took on life. Even though it cost us a lot, it made us a lot. I won't sit here and write about having done it right or wrong; we all have our own life path. I will just reiterate how we learned our lessons in the fire. We took the trial-and-error route by insisting that we learn these lessons ourselves and bullfighting our way to the top.

I will tell you that you don't have to work yourself to the bone and brink of exhaustion to attain your goals and dreams. In the upcoming portion of this book, I am going to teach you some more health-conscious approaches to making your millions. I also hope to help you enjoy the process a bit more than we got to, but also, take heed.

We had a handful of mentors telling us how to 'do it right' and still insisted on paving our own way. You have every right to go about this process however you want. I just hope to tell you enough stories about trial and tribulation to encourage you to take a different route.

In the long run, we learned how to slow down. We learned how to care for ourselves. We learned how to pace ourselves and we also began to diversify. Before we head into part three of this book, I want to leave you with a brief list of some lessons I learned from the fire of some of the biggest challenges we faced. If I can spare anyone even a bit of hardship, I will feel I have done my job on this planet.

Lessons from the Hard Times:

Due Diligence- Study your subject and take everything into consideration before tackling something new. I wish we would've talked to ten banks prior to taking on our subdivision project or met with private investors. I could have saved eighteen months of meetings and $150,000 toward hiring engineers and attorneys only to find out banks weren't going to lend us any money. If we had spent more time studying the project as opposed to starting it, we would have known we couldn't start it.

Humbleness- Getting your ass kicked is humbling. Don't act like a baller until you actually are a baller. *Fake it until you make it* isn't true and just more often makes you feel like an idiot in the end. What happens when you fake it is you get stuck maintaining the facade and that becomes daunting work. There are other, more aligned ways to practice manifestation.

Darkness- The devil is always lurking. He is lurking behind people who post terrible things about you online and lurking in the darkness of your most negative thoughts about yourself. Learning about the darkness was enough for me to never want to go there again. It's good not to be scared of it but that doesn't mean we are meant to linger there. I trust that if we go through hard times again, I will be better prepared without falling into the dark hole that the devil loves to invite us into.

Ask for Guidance- There is a difference between guidance and a bail-out. You learn more from figuring it out than being saved or rescued. We had an amazing mentor who could've bailed us out financially when the subdivision fell through but he didn't. Instead, he guided us and told us different things to try. He made us do the work. He stood with us while we learned a lesson first hand that we will never forget or have to repeat. We took his advice, tried different things, and learned much more than if he would've saved us.

Feel-Good Mindset- Do something that makes you feel good to boost your mindset. You need to feel good in order to keep feeling good. When I booked that trip to Hawaii on credit cards, I didn't know how we were going to pay for it, but I knew I needed something to look forward to in order to get me through the hardest year of my life. That trip saved our relationship and in turn helped us feel good, have fun, and forget about our troubles for a second. It helped us reset our intentions and when we started out a new year we were ready to do better and figure things out with a new and improved mindset shift.

Talk to God- Don't believe the devil and anything he's spewing. It will get better. Ask God for help. Ask for divine guidance. Tell the devil to buzz off. Something to keep in mind is that you have a direct line to God. It is called prayer. You can get into an immediate conversation with God and ask for the help, guidance, and support you need.

Books- Read books about entrepreneurs. Glean from their stories. They all went through challenges to gain success. There really are these initiation experiences we all go through on the path to success. Don't think you are going to just dive in, skip over any tough challenges, and come out on top. I am all for your success, but you will face your own set of challenges and I would bet money that there is a book already written about the challenges you will face. Books are the most affordable access you have to your favorite coaches, leaders, and mentors and are a great place to start.

Write the Check- Watch the movie, *The Secret* or read the book, *The Magic* and write yourself a check for all the money you want and need. Add to the description line getting paid for work you love. Have a simulation where you take that check to the bank to cash it. Start feeling yourself into the abundant lifestyle you dream about. Especially the one where you get paid to be you.

Gratitude- There is nothing that will change your mindset quicker than feeling overwhelmed with gratitude. When you are overwhelmed with stress or anxiety, your best bet is to go back to the basics of gratitude. The more you can simplify, the better. This will get you out of your worried head and back into your reality. Start small and get bigger. Start with your breath, your clothes, the clean water you are drinking, electricity, your home, anything. Think about what you're grateful for and sit in the feeling of how grateful you are for those things. You must remember how blessed you are to become more blessed. More things to be grateful for will come, I promise.

Part 3

Chapter 12

Breaking the Mold

"By leaning into the discomfort of the unknown
and saying yes to faith, we created the life of our dreams."

No one, and I mean no one, can cause more destruction in less than two minutes than a two-year-old avoiding a diaper change.

Once a toddler realizes that someone is threatening to come after him with a bag of wipes, it's game on. It takes one quick glance and he's gone. To dodge a new diaper, he's throwing toy tractors, skid loaders, legos and anything he can find behind him to create an obstacle on his mad dash around the house.

No one really wants to chase a little human around to change their stinky backside so Noah and I had to get creative in settling the score for who would have to go into battle. In our travels all over the world, we have found that the most diplomatic way to settle the challenge of who must do the deed is playing rock-paper-scissors.

I pretty much always won, so in his defeat, Noah would set out on his quest to clean up our kiddos. Our babes would eventually surrender their resistance to a fresh rear but not without a fight. Thank goodness, we always won in the end, in parenting and life.

Noah and I have used the game of rock-paper-scissors many times throughout our relationship and business to settle who must be the one to perform an undesirable task or make a call that neither of us wants to make. Calls where we had to let a homeowner know that there was a price increase for lumber for their home or a delay in product that would put the home building schedule behind by a month. We honor the outcome of R-P-S and get the job done. However, there have been plenty of times when we had to put all the games aside and just step into the unknown together as a team.

We have both been known to be jack of all trades. As an ag teacher, I was teaching everything from horticulture to veterinary science to biotechnology to small gas engines. Noah was the secretary, salesperson, and serviceman of his landscaping business. In the homebuilding industry, general contractors are generally referred to as the jack of all trades because you very literally need to know about all the trade jobs. You need to know the full range of work, so you know who to call for what project. This also helped in our real estate investing business when we would be running numbers on deals ranging from commercial warehouses, to apartment buildings, or mobile home communities. Our general contracting experience came in handy to know the going rate of labor in the trades, so we weren't getting extravagantly upcharged. This made us very diverse in the work we could do.

I am sure you have heard the phrase, *just because you can, doesn't mean you have to.* Well, just because you can do it all, doesn't mean you *should.* Just because we knew a little bit about a lot of things didn't mean we should have been doing all the hands-on work ourselves. Our ambition got the best of us, and we found ourselves competing in rock-paper-scissors more frequently as time went on.

Good, bad, or otherwise, we made a lot of our work very hands-on. We learned that being heavily involved in our own homebuilding company seemed to slow us down in expanding our real estate investing business which was our ultimate end goal. We thought we were doing ourselves a favor and saving money by being the general contractor, real estate broker, home designer, customer relations manager, human resources department, social media, and marketing department all on our own. It is a great way to get started in learning the tools of the trade but if you keep it up, it can hold you up in progressing as fast as you'd like and it's not entirely necessary. We did learn how to do it all. However, it has also burned us out and stretched us too thin.

This was a significant learning curve for us. As investors, we were meant to be the visionaries and supervisors of the projects, not the trade laborers hammering nails and laying tile. Early in our real estate investing courses, our instructors taught us to hire our 'dream team.' Your dream team would consist of people such as a real estate agent, banker, insurance agent, lawyer, bookkeeper, accountant, general contractor, property manager, carpenter, and a handyman helper.

Here in the Midwest, people believe in hard work. We grew up believing in being involved, *leading by example.* We believed, and still do, that part of leadership is walking the talk. I did, however, tend to take that belief to a bit of an extreme. It influenced my mentality of always having to prove that I could outwork someone I might be in competition with. This desire to prove ourselves came from the value of our credibility. There is a sense of dignity in diligently putting in the work.

Stories that start with the hero in the trenches have a certain heartwarming relatability that people appreciate. Everyone loves an underdog. Having *been through* it shows a level of experience that establishes trust. There is a level of respect and understanding that comes when others know that you've 'been there, done that.' We know this to be true, but we didn't hurl ourselves into the trenches just to show off, we wanted to get the full-range experience because we valued hard work and much as the next red-blooded American.

Of course, there is a certain level of confidence I have because of the work I have taken on. I can't be fooled or ripped off, in the building process or in the industry. In the real estate investing indus-try, there are handfuls of people out there who open their mouths and sound like an infomercial. There's all these 'Get Rich Quick,' 'We Buy Ugly Houses,' or 'Fix or Flop' shows that trap hopeful people into a scam. You hear podcasts and commercials about people that are going to teach you all the secrets of becoming a real estate millionaire. It all just sounds sleazy after a while, especially if you have an ear for it.

A lot of information you will find is being put out by people who don't have first-hand experience. A good portion of the people presenting themselves as experts worked for giant firms and haven't practiced what they preach. Noah and I tend to roll our eyes when we hear those infomercial folks promising riches and preying on people looking for a legitimate way to reach financial freedom. They aren't as credible in our perspective because it is clear they haven't been out in the world, bootstrapping and figuring it out for themselves.

We are 'from the ground, up' kind of people. We started from scratch and knew what it means to build your dreams with your own bare hands. I am telling so many success and failure stories in this book because I want to share the real journey we've been on. There are plenty of great leaders and courses out there, but you really want to listen to your gut when it comes to picking a mentor. If they seem sleazy or you feel pressure from some 'limited time offer' it is likely you are being taken for a fool. I believe that if I don't share the information that I have learned, I am doing a disservice to God and you.

I know that if I did not morph from hands-on contractor and investor into the author, teacher, leader, educator, motivator, inspirational figure that I am, I would not have been living out my true purpose. I believe that everything I have been through has all been for a reason. There is a reason I endured the traumas and hardships I've gone through. There is a reason I became a fighter. In my recovery from burnout, I have realized how I am here to be a beacon of light, hope, peace, and love. I couldn't be my true and full self by running myself ridiculously ragged. It is by standing in my truth that I can make the difference that I came to make.

We started our business and became entrepreneurs to be free. We wanted to be our own bosses. This was all new to me and sounded so exciting and my passion and ambition took over. We had to prove ourselves, so we set sail on creating this business and life of freedom. Over the years, we realized that we had not set up our business to be one of 'freedom' and instead we ended up with a business that we felt enslaved to.

Rather than having a forty-hour-per-week job, we created an eighty-hour-per-week business. At the beginning, we were eager to succeed so we met with people from eight am to eight pm, seven days per week if necessary. We had no one else to rely on to make it all happen so we took it all on ourselves. We didn't think this was an issue at first because we desperately wanted to make the business work. We would do anything for the customer, including skipping out on time with our own family, celebrating our anniversary, seeing friends, and doing anything fun that wasn't considered 'productive.'

With guilty hearts, we admittedly didn't see much of our daughter in her first year of life. It's only in retrospect that we know better. We learned the hard way. We had to suffer from the costs of those sacrifices. I could give you endless examples of how hard we pushed ourselves, but I am pretty sure you get it. I am sure you have some examples in your own life of how far you've gone for success. I am willing to guess that if you could have done it better, easier, faster, and smarter, you would have.

We worried that because we were so involved and 'head down' in our own business that we potentially missed out on so many greater opportunities out there. We worried that maybe we could've been further, been faster; that life could've been so much easier for us if we would've just looked up occasionally. It put a pit in our stomachs when we realized the cost of our hustle mindset.

In fact, we learned that the 'hustle' mindset was a burnout mindset. This doesn't mean that you don't have to still show up. If you want success, you still need to show up for it and put in effort toward taking aligned actions. What we didn't realize is that for the effort we were putting in, rest and recovery was also needed to counter that. We were in such a never-let-up mindset that we didn't, until we broke.

We knew deep down that we were worn out. We couldn't continue to do the job of multiple people each without help. It stopped us dead in our tracks. We accepted that we needed to make serious, intentional shifts to the life we were living and the way we were doing business. This became the time we decided to move in a different direction with our homebuilding company. We were known as one of the best homebuilding companies in our area and yet, we decided it was time to figure out how to maximize our growth while maximizing enjoyment of life.

Being at the top of our game and realizing the business that we created was no longer serving us felt like a hard pill to swallow at first. We knew we needed to pivot though we didn't know what that looked like yet. We know it wasn't all for nothing because of all the lessons we learned that we now get to share with you, but at the time, we felt miserable about it. In the process of building our business, we lost ourselves. We lost our happiness, excitement, and enthusiasm for life.

Once we woke up from that nightmare, we set out on a mission to find ourselves, be who we wanted to be, and do what we wanted to do. We had to face the fact that our health, wealth, and happiness depended on it. When we did, we pivoted and began to find joy in our work again. We found ourselves again.

Collectively, we are coming up to a different era than past generations. The hustle and grind culture is on its way out. Hustling yourself into exhaustion is not as admirable as it used to be and it is definitely not a sustainable way to grow a business. We are at the phase of its extinction where it is 'adapt or die.' Shift your mode of operation to flow over force or be forced into extinction through exhaustion. We decided to adapt.

As soon as we decided to adjust, suddenly, dozens of requests began to come in and we were saying 'no' to them. In the spring of 2021, we turned away nearly one hundred requests for custom home builds. The first few times that we said 'no' to income put that same pit in our stomachs. We were saying 'no' to that kind of hustle, but we were saying 'yes' to the next step of our success. We were saying 'yes' to leveling up. Luckily, this wasn't our first go around on this type of uplevel.

When Noah decided to quit his landscaping company to start a homebuilding company, he had the same pit feeling in his gut. When he started saying 'no' to landscaping clients, he was saying 'no' to making an easy five-thousand-dollar profit for a job. You may be able to relate in your own way but when you have a family to support, turning away such an income opportunity feels crazy.

However, when he said 'no' to a five-thousand-dollar landscaping job, those 'no's turned into yeses for thirty to fifty thousand dollars of profit for homebuilding jobs. Once we started saying 'no' to fifty thousand per homebuilding jobs, we were saying 'yes' to more real estate investing transactions. We were averaging five hundred thousand to a million dollars in equity per project. Our 'no's have led to better 'yes's, but we had to become willing to adapt, adjust, and trust.

We also had to adjust our hard work mentality. It is easy to overwork ourselves in any industry, so we had to break the mold of our hustle and grind pride. We had to shift away from pushing every boundary to enjoying the process and growth in a healthy way. This took mental and emotional work that we will dig into in this portion of the book. I will guide you through an inner evolution that will help you to break the mold you were born into.

Too many people stay 'comfortably uncomfortable' in life. They convince themselves they are happy. They convince themselves that staying small is better than taking risks and reaching for true joy. If I would've gotten used to hating my day-to-day tasks at my previous employment for the sake of staying comfortable, I would have grown even more resentful and depleted. Instead of staying where you are for the purpose of staying comfortable, I challenge you to make the necessary adjustments. Stretch out of your comfort zone for greater joy and fulfillment.

Because we started adjusting, we had bigger rewards. What felt like risky noes turned into lucrative yesses. Our new success was no accident. We reached new heights because we began walking a new path.

To kick it up a notch, we finally started taking more time to be proud, happy, and grateful. We took more time for enjoyment, relaxation, rest, and fun. We took more time for celebration and kept manifesting easier ways to make money. We have shifted our mindsets away from grit and grinding to growth and gratitude. We proved to ourselves that there are better ways to grow a business and we are committed to teaching you those ways.

We get to be proud of what we have built. We had a goal of making a million dollars and we did. We set out to teach other people about financial freedom through our books, podcasts, courses, teaching, and we are. We committed to being wealthy *and* healthy and it's only because of changing our approach that we can say we get to have both.

We are manifesting the life of our dreams because we broke the mold. We released self-deprecating habits and patterns and learned that success can be fast, easy, and fun. By leaning into the discomfort of the unknown and saying yes with faith, we created the life of our dreams. In this part of the book, I am going to help you break the mold and reform your mindset into one of growth, gratitude, abundance, joy and success. Let's get after it.

Chapter 13

Breaking the Chains

"You do not have to suffer your way through life. You do not have to solely survive this lifetime. You can authentically thrive in it."

Of the millions that I have earned and spent; healing work is by far the best investment I have ever made. I am teaching you about financial freedom but that comes from mental, emotional, and spiritual freedom. Your dreams come when you wake up from your nightmares.

I learned that healing your mind and heart is the true path to healing your body. Your financial freedom is related because you are a holistic being. My journey to break the chains of my past led me to lay a sturdy foundation for my future. As the years went on, I evolved my way through an education they don't teach in school. I made it my business to take on the inner work. I dropped out of the school of hard knocks and assigned myself a masters in self-mastery.

For most of my life, I unconsciously struggled with the trauma I endured, and it was when I met the devil in the darkness of my depression that I decided to pick myself up and start out on a new course. I wanted to start taking control of my own life. It wasn't perfect in that first year, but at least I was trying something new. I desired success and happiness, but I had lost my faith and needed a redirection. I dove into books, podcasts, and as much research as I could get my hands on. I became more intentional about that redirection, and I could tell a shift was happening.

As I was reading, listening, and learning, I started to really comprehend the toxicity within my family relationships. I had mostly adapted to *the way my family was* but the more I studied, the wider my eyes were opened. I was never afraid to speak up about the injustices I witnessed but I had never really made any measurable adjustments in my youth. Sure, I got away to college and one summer internship in Montana but that was just creating distance between me and the problem. I never really addressed it.

What I was learning in the personal and professional development work I had taken on started me on a path of setting boundaries *and* maintaining them. I started making changes and demands; some were met, most were not. This put a strain on those relationships. I finally cut ties with my dad and one month later, found out I was pregnant with my daughter, Tesla, whom I affectionately refer to as the *testing Tesla*.

I remember specifically visualizing having a daughter in my younger years. I imagined having a shot at parenting properly and giving her a life I only ever dreamed about. If you ask either of my parents, they will tell you that we had the best childhood a kid could ever have. Yes, we had a lot of creature comforts, but they both seem to forget screaming, shrieks of terror, slapping, stomping, shuffling, angry voices, constant tension, guilt trips, and more. They don't seem to understand the direct and indirect impact of their behaviors, but I wanted a chance to correct that. More specifically, I wanted to end the cycle. I wanted to break the chains of generational abuse and trauma that plagues my lineage. I wasn't going to let that abuse linger any longer. I was going to put it to rest.

And then potty training started…

I call her testing Tesla because she tests every bit of my self-proclaimed healing journey. When Tesla started potty training, I would get so angry with her and yell. I would behave dominantly, and that energy was affecting her and my husband. One night, during a potty-training meltdown, my husband looked at me very seriously and said, "your dad is coming out."

That reflection stopped me in my tracks and practically knocked the breath out of me. I couldn't see in it my rage, but I knew it the moment he said it. It turned me into a puddle of tears. I had to face my reflection in the mirror and realize that I was starting to mirror what I had seen growing up. It came out without me knowing.

I knew I always wanted to end the cycle and then there I was starting to repeat it. My daughter and I were at odds with each other, and I wanted nothing more than to love her wholly and unconditionally. Parenting in general is challenging but when you have an upbringing that teaches you manipulation, reactivity, and explosive anger, that stuff gets stuck inside of you. Then, it comes out when you are challenged and feeling helpless.

I was committed to having a close-knit family which wasn't going to be possible if I continued being angry and reactive all the time. I wanted to be a better mother. The night Noah called me out on my anger, with tears in my eyes, I went online and found a therapist. I was so upset that I just picked one off a random website and booked a session.

I attended my first therapy session at thirty-five years old. Relatively, this may seem old or young to you for a first therapy session, but I realized I had three decades worth of repressed memories and energy pushing their way out. I couldn't have described it that way when I first started, but as I unpacked it all, more kept coming up and out, both childhood trauma and my birthing traumas. At first, each session took a lot out of me, and I would need to rest for the remainder of the day to recover. I could tell this was just the beginning.

Therapy brought up everything I had stored away for decades. Once I got a real experience of this work, I accepted that I couldn't afford to *not* do therapy. I learned a lot during this phase of my life. I learned how I played the rescuer role in the 'trauma triangle' for a long time. I learned what gaslighting was. I learned what guilt, shame, and fear truly do to people. I learned about the role that emotions play on so many memories. The lessons were endless, and the breakthroughs were invaluable.

Therapy, holistic healing practices, energy work, and coaching are tools I will continue for the rest of my life, and I recommend them to everyone. As we continue through this chapter, I am going to explain different modalities of healing work and all of them have their purpose and impact. Taking an aligned approach at different phases is important so with some distinction, you may be able to sense which ones are right for you.

In my humble opinion, everyone needs some form of therapy. Everyone has emotional baggage to unpack and talking it out with your friends or family can only get you so far. I highly value and recommend professional support to take on such sensitive and vulnerable work. There are stigmas and ignorance that put a barrier between people and the help they need, and I hope to normalize some new options for you.

I am very driven to share this because, in my upbringing, it was not common practice to go to therapy, coaching or get help. It was hardly a practice to admit that you needed help. Suffering was more normal or accepted than healing. It was even admired. That work hard ethic had its subtle effects in every area of life, not just career or school.

I had to learn that it's okay to ask for help. It's okay to call a therapist. It's okay to get support. Something that I learned along the way is that it's okay to trust people. This was a challenge for me because I defaulted to being an independent person for survival. I had to spend time deconditioning all the survival tactics I had learned for my own protection. Therapy will reveal what there is to work on and it becomes your job to accept the shift.

Once I began the work, I started feeling different from the inside out. Things that used to upset me didn't trigger me anymore, or if they did, I could move through the wave of reactivity more quickly. I learned how to prevent spiraling and turning a speck of dust into a giant tornado. This turned me into someone I liked. I began seeing the benefits everywhere and my health improved as a result.

I believe going to therapy or coaching should be as common as going to the chiropractor. It should be like visiting your hair stylist or the dentist. Working on your mental health and inner self is just as important as working on your physical self.

The route of therapy opened a whole new world to me that I had never realized was available. However, my journey toward learning more about alternative healthcare was just beginning. There are countless options that have been around for centuries, and newer methods being developed every year. There is something for everyone to clear their past and step boldly into their future.

I started with therapy, but it also opened my awareness to other work in the world. I started to hear the term 'inner work' more frequently as time went on. I am referring to a type of healing that comes after you've been working on healing past traumas with a therapist or another professional. Working in a therapy or counseling format tends to 'surface' repressed memories and emotions to process and release. It comes up and out in groves and there isn't much more to do then see and feel it all, but this phase doesn't last forever.

Sooner or later, you start to feel clearer, and this allows you to practice the inner work with more focus and intention. When you clear the body of all the stored trauma and emotions, you become liberated mentally, emotionally, intellectually, physically, and spiritually. Once I experienced the 'emptying' of my trauma, I felt a lot of new aches and pains in my body.

I haven't explicitly said this so far, but I have a medical rap sheet about a mile long. I have 'isms' and 'itises' that would put even the strongest person on bed rest. The physical pain I have dealt with has often laid me out for the count.

From broken bones, falling out of cars, concussions, asthma, chronic bronchitis, back problems, hip issues, nerve damage, pre-eclampsia, to high blood pressure, I am walking medical wonder. I am giving you the cliff notes version of my medical history but let's just say it's always something. I struggled so much in my youth that I even wrote my own will at age thirteen. Eventually, I became so conditioned to pain that I thought it was just life. I even learned to numb most of it out.

Once I started to heal in therapy, my body pain began communicating with me. My body, mind, and soul couldn't take the cycle of abuse any longer. As I started to heal myself, being around my parents activated pain in my body that became impossible to ignore. I would experience physical pain before their physical presence was even known. This became my responsibility to handle.

The majority of physical ailments you experience are a direct result of an emotional imbalance. That was a tough concept for me to take in. My body was creating physical pain and illness to grab my attention and show me what emotional wounds were left unhealed. I began to research each physical ailment I had and which emotional discord it aligned with. It was alarming how accurately this information lined up with what was happening to me. Staying attuned to my body has been, and continues to be, a lifelong journey for me, but it was the inner work that taught me that healing the heart and mind also heals the ailments of the body.

We have been trained to think that modern science has the cure for everything. However, in my experience, I have found that isn't completely true. So often, Western medicine treats the symptom, not the source. This can become a real problem when suffering with and attempting to resolve chronic or recurring health issues. In my own journey, I set out to understand more about the connection between mind, spirit, and body.

As the layers were getting peeled back and I was going deeper into the holistic healing approach, I found energy workers, reiki masters, acupuncturists, and many others who helped me alleviate long-standing issues that no pill could cure. I came to understand more about how the body stores emotional pain as physical pain. If I wanted to have a truly healed body, I needed to have a fully healed mind, so I started a serious journey to heal every aspect of my life.

Setting out to heal every aspect of my life put me on an unexpected journey that tore the doors off my energetic expansion. I found a business coach who led with a beautiful mixture of soul, strategy, and spirituality. It wasn't coaching based on traditional business strategy. It was based on inner work and now that I felt empowered in that arena, it felt like a perfectly aligned next step.

The connections I created in this new coaching community were with other leaders who were talking about time freedom as much as I valued financial freedom. I hadn't ever really considered time freedom before, but it made perfect sense to me the moment I heard it. It felt like I had found something I didn't know I lost. Something I kept hearing in all this talk about freedom was that it was eighty percent inner work. This also made perfect sense to me, but went against everything I knew about hard work, hustle, and grit. I saw what inner work there was for me to do next; break the chains of back breaking work.

I knew about manifestation, visualization, and the Law of Attraction. I understood that the mind can achieve what it conceives but for some reason I hadn't made that connection with the inner work I had been doing. This soul and spirit inspired approach was different from the personal and professional development work I had gotten from courses and books. This style of coaching was based on flow, divine guidance, and aligning your higher self for clarity and direction.

As time went on in my coaching work, we talked more about meditation, connecting to your higher self, and connecting to God. We talked about looking inward and listening to your body wisdom and becoming quiet so you could hear the communications of your heart and soul. I had begun to understand how critical the phases of therapy and inner work were and how they led me to this phase of being more available for channeling such downloads. If I were still as 'foggy' as before I started my healing journey, I wouldn't be available for the new levels I knew I was reaching.

Prior to this program I had not really done much meditation. I didn't really know what meditation was. Quite frankly, I used to think meditation was hokey or *woo woo*. I never really gave meditation serious thought and only tried it a few random times when I was feeling down and out. I tried it more out of desperation than as a true practice. I told myself that I didn't have time for it but really, I didn't take time for it. After being trained and encouraged in my program, I started to make time and it became an essential part of my well-being practices.

I am at a point in my health journey that if I don't meditate, I don't feel aligned, and if I don't feel aligned, my whole day feels off and things spiral from there. I have gotten away from and come back to meditation enough times to prove to myself that consistency and commitment is the key to success in this area. Nowadays, I meditate every morning. I prioritize waking up and intentionally greeting the day. I grab my journal to head outside to sit on my meditation bench with a cup of tea by my side or meditate, pray, and speak affirmations as I go for a morning walk.

This more mindful approach to living has produced a life that I don't always need healing from. Between the inner work, and giving up hard work and hustle, I started to level out in a way that made me feel more consistently centered, focused, and grounded. The more inner work I did, the more clarity and emotional freedom I was experiencing.

When I started working with these business coaches, they talked about God a lot. We talked about alignment with God and aligning with your soul and spirit guidance. They prioritized zooming out and taking a thirty-thousand-foot perspective of your life. This helped to align with what my soul was nudging me to do. This became a practice in understanding my intuition which led to something even more divine. This program opened my heart back up to God.

I grew up going to church with my family but never really felt deeply connected to God. My parents were upstanding members of the church and our family followed suit. We were regular attendees. We were regular donors of a frequently high amount in the offering plate.

The ironic part is how my parents lived their lives outside of church services. We would hardly be able to make it into the car before they were arguing about something. It was constant. The only time they weren't arguing was when we were in public and were 'making face.'

I can remember sitting in the back of the car blurting out in the middle of their argument, "Didn't you hear *anything* that was said in today's message?" They were not living their life in alignment with God. They were not living in love. They were not in love. Their marriage was like a quiet volcano, beautiful on the outside but extremely hot volcanic lava brewed and bubbled on the inside ready to burst at any moment.

After going away to college, I rarely went to church. I only went here and there when I was home on the weekends. I didn't really know what I thought about church. I still prayed and talked to God. I still held onto the idea of God being part of me, but my faith dwindled. It dwindled as I saw my parents' marriage fall apart. I wondered what Truth, if any, was out there. I wondered if all 'church' was about was pretending to be holy. For most of my life, I felt God's presence outside of church. I felt closer to God when I went for a walk outside. I used to feel God's love in nature, in the valleys on our family farm, and in the mountains of Montana. To me, God was in the nature around me as opposed to just in the four walls of church.

When I started working with these coaches and their community, God became so much more real to me. I want to keep this fluid for whatever Higher Power you connect with. That may be Spirit, Universe, etc. Mostly, I am directly connecting with Jesus and other times it is who I believe are my guardian angels. No matter who or what it is in any given prayer or meditation session, I honor the presence, connection, and guidance.

This has been my own path toward experiencing a fully healed mind and body. Some of this might not resonate with you. Take what resonates and leave the rest. For most, there is spiritual healing before there can be spiritual expansion. This is where I would recommend starting with therapy and shifting as you become lighter.

Particularly in my work with this coaching community, I felt more connected to a Higher Power than ever before. Now, I talk to God daily. Sometimes twice daily. Sometimes all day long. It has become necessary to meditate and take time to listen to what God wants to tell me. I sit silent to listen. I ask questions. I feel so in alignment that

I am in an ongoing conversation with God, asking Him for guidance and sharing what I'm grateful for.

In these conversations, I ask God to release all negative thoughts, emotions, and toxicity from my body and I focus on letting go of the pain, tension, stress, anger, resentment, and judgments that I hold in my body. I ask God to lift my burdens. I actively practice blessing and releasing that which no longer serves me. I call in all my desires. I ask for clarity and conviction. In return, I feel filled with peace, love, joy, and light. I sense a light so bright that it permeates everything and everyone around and lifts everything and everyone up with me. Everything else falls away.

I feel some of the most flow and connectedness when I am sharing what I'm grateful for and what I desire in my life as if I already have it. Prayer and meditation open me up to feeling the feelings that I desire. I can sense the co-creation I am participating in and it raises my frequency. As I feel them more fully, I experience those feelings through physical manifestations. This is the peace and healing I'd like to share with you.

If you focus on your own body for a moment, I am wondering if you can notice the frequency rising within you from reading this chapter. I am sharing information that would give you access to a newer you, a lighter you. Without actively calling it out, it can easily go unnoticed. I am asking you to focus your attention on your inner world and tap into your soul self for a moment.

Because I understand our oneness, I can tell you that your soul is dancing for you to be reading this information and awakening to all that is available and possible for you. You do not have to suffer your way through life. You do not have to solely survive this lifetime. You can authentically thrive in it. There is a happiness and joy awakening in you, in all of us, as we raise the Collective frequency of humanity. That starts with healing and progresses through the work I have been sharing here.

I won't say that I'm completely healed. Healing is a lifelong process. I am a different person than I was a day, a year, or a decade ago.

I became a better mom, wife, business partner, and person because I took on my inner work. I don't get as triggered anymore. What used to trigger me for days and weeks flows through me in a matter of hours or less now. I can process more rapidly and without as much aftermath and clean-up.

There have been times along my journey that I have felt the desire to 'be done' healing and transforming, but I want to tell you that for as long as you are breathing, you are growing. For as long as you are living, you have the responsibility of healing, releasing, and forgiving. I share this to encourage you to accept the constant growth you are faced with. When we resist it, we make it harder for ourselves and that is when we experience suffering.

I used to resent, hide, avoid, and sugarcoat my past. I used to damn my parents for all the healing I have felt plagued with. Now, I can express gratitude for everything I've gone through. I thank God for every single person, experience, and lesson. I also thank God for being patient and gracious with me as I finally found my way back to our daily talks. It's good to be back in my connection with God. I am back, better than ever, and always raising my frequency.

At this juncture, I want to remind you that we co-create our reality. I say remind because you know this on some level. You recognize this Truth beyond the physical realm. I have learned that if I want to truly create a life of freedom, I need to release so much of the resistance and belief systems that I had grown up with. I have to deprogram the idea that life is a battle, and we are all alone. This required more trust than I started out with when I began my healing journey.

I needed to surrender to flow and believe that everything I desired was already there waiting for me. Have you ever heard the statement *ask and you shall receive?* That is the representation of co-creation. When you put your desire out there, your Higher Power begins a perfect storm to manifest that desire in your life. This is something I continue to practice and work on. It is a powerful truth of creating all of the freedom you desire.

You cannot co-create and find your way to your desires if you are muddled up with your anger, hatred, and resentments. They cloud your head and fog your vision. No matter where you are on your healing journey, keep going. It is when you peel and peel and peel those layers of jadedness off that you become available for the intuitive guidance that will walk you right up to your desires or drop them in your lap.

Manifestation isn't the hard part. The challenge lies with breaking the chains of the past. If you are reading this book, you have been tasked with breaking the mold, the chains, and the rules that have kept you small and safe. This work isn't just about you. It is for the future generations, that they may have a better starting point than us. It is raising the Collective health, wealth, and well-being.

I know that your drive for financial freedom has to do with the highest good of all because you would not have made it to this page of this book if your success wasn't meant to come from a heart-centered place. There are plenty of ways to become rich. Your wealth will come from your mental, emotional, physical, and spiritual health. Keep the faith in why you are here and keep healing while that becomes clear.

Chapter 14

Breaking the Rules

"Creating your dream life and manifesting your desires will require you going so far outside your comfort zone that you become unrecognizable to yourself and others."

I am a rule-breaker. At this point, if I see a rule coming my way, I mostly consider how to bend or break it. Not strictly to be difficult, but because I believe in creativity and possibility. I believe in diversity and ingenuity. Some of the rules I have broken are:

- "Get a secure job"
- "You can't break up the family"
- "It's going to be a battle"
- "This is the right way to do things"
- "You can't parent like that"
- "Business isn't done that way"
- "Behave, or else…"

I love the way Laurel Thatcher Ulrich says, "well-behaved women rarely make history." I agree. There would be no innovation without revolution. If we never questioned the rules, bucked the system, or rocked the boat, we'd still be living the life of cavemen, foraging for our own food.

Don't get me wrong, I don't mind foraging, but I also love modern day farming machinery to get the job done as well. Evolution is a natural phenomenon. It has occurred for all of time and will continue forever with or without humans, but it has been the thought leaders and innovators of humanity that have helped us evolve as a species. It is the people who challenge *the way it is* who come up with new, more efficient ways and creations who help us move forward faster. As you may have noticed, these people aren't always the most popular, at least not at first.

It may be upsetting to those who know you a certain way to then watch you change into someone that no longer meets their expectations. It will frustrate them to become someone they cannot control. It will be especially confrontational when you challenge their belief systems, rules, and requirements.

What I hope to provide for you is permission to break the 'rules.' I want to offer you the invitation to start questioning what keeps you limited. It may seem difficult. It may feel scary, dangerous, irresponsible, disrespectful, and more. I can tell you from experience that breaking the mold, the chains, and the rules can feel vulnerable and uncomfortable, but not as uncomfortable as staying in the boxes that other people try to fit you into.

Disappointing others often meant prioritizing myself, and the more I did this, the more self-love I experienced. I reaped more rewarding results when I took this risk, and it paid off enough times that I learned it was for the best. I wasn't always great at putting myself first. It took trying and failing plenty of times to get better at breaking the rules that kept me small.

As you begin to wake up to this idea, you will see that many of the rules you follow don't make a whole lot of sense for you and your life. They may have always just been there, dictating, but now that you are giving everything a second consideration, you can see how you were blindly adapting to a restriction that wasn't in your best interest. As you start to reevaluate the rules you are following, you may ask yourself questions like:

- Whose rules?
- What rules?

- Rules from when?
- Rules from where?
- According to who?

Taking these questions into consideration may start to peel back the layers on the way you've been conditioned to behave a certain way and obey or submit to a lifestyle you don't necessarily agree with. Waking up is the first step. The second step is appropriate action, otherwise known as *follow-through*.

Not every thought leader has followed through on their brilliant thoughts. Not every great idea sees the light of day. Many people who question and doubt systems stay quiet and follow suit instead of acting on them. Unfortunately, a larger majority of people stay dreamers instead of doers.

There are millions of dreams that die with their dreamer, and it is time we change that. Realizing your visions in this lifetime is reserved for the ones who have taken inspired and aligned action. Creating your dream life and manifesting your desires will require you going so far outside of your comfort zone that you become unrecognizable to yourself and others.

I became unrecognizable to myself and my family when I walked away from my relationship with my dad. I became unpopular when I threatened the happy family image and structure. I caused a lot of turmoil when I called out what was happening behind closed doors. I was blamed for being intolerant when I questioned the abuse and manipulation, but none of that stopped me from prioritizing my health, well-being, and success.

I want to add an important part of 'boundary setting' that often gets overlooked. Boundaries are about love, for yourself and the other people involved. Yes, you are likely protecting yourself, but you are also helping someone else break a toxic behavior. Tolerating something inappropriate is enabling them to be an abuser. Boundaries aren't comfortable but they can be very necessary and that doesn't always mean you hate the person. Quite the opposite, you are practicing an incredible amount of strength to draw a hard line and stick to it.

This practice will also tell you how to address the situation moving forward. When you set a boundary, and the person repeatedly disregards and crosses it, you will find out very quickly how much they value you and themselves. This is not for you to judge; it is for you to respect and honor. I have chosen to walk away from both of my parents at times because they didn't respect my boundaries and standards. They were welcome in my life on my terms and when that was constantly being compromised, it became my responsibility to handle.

There will most certainly be people who honor your boundaries, standards, and expectations but it is you that must set and maintain them. You do not have to throw everyone on the chopping block every time they challenge you. You must practice discernment when deciding who has access to you and how much access they are permitted. This is where you start making your own rules. This is where you really stop following what everyone else says and decide what you say is good for yourself and your life.

One thing I can tell you is that being a rule-breaker can feel like a lonely road. When you are breaking away from everything you once knew, you naturally pay more attention to the loss than the potential gain. This happens particularly because the risk doesn't guarantee the reward, but as I have shared, I was always willing to find out. Being willing to break the rules has helped me manifest my most abundant life. That became clear to me when I risked my loneliness for my beliefs…or for my nonbelief.

Noah and I have often bucked the trend and gone against the grain whether that be the way we got married, how we ran our businesses to how we raised our children.

When we got married, I knew that I wanted to get married on my family farm. It was my dream and together it became our dream. At the time of our marriage, outdoor weddings and farm weddings weren't the favorable way to get married. Many frowned upon the idea all together saying it wasn't the proper way to get married. We were the pioneers of outdoor farm weddings at the time and had to stand our ground for our dreams to come true. People didn't know what to wear to an outdoor farm wedding or how it would work. It didn't matter to me what anyone else thought if Noah and I were happy in our decision.

Our wedding day was a perfect September day in 2011 on my family farm where Noah wore an ivory suit, and I wore an ivory lace dress. The day was filled with September sunshine, horse drawn wagon rides, a ceremony in the valley and a bluegrass band at the farm shed reception afterward. We danced our hearts out. It was an amazing night to remember.

We are so glad we stood our ground and did what made sense to us. The important thing to note is that we did this together as a team. We chose each other, we had each other's back and decided to do what was right for us no matter what anyone else told us.

As we started a business and family together, we continued to break the rules. I have told you a lot about our stubbornness in business and how we bucked most of the rules and guidelines for success just to prove ourselves right, but in parenthood, we took a more natural approach. When it comes to parenting, we both follow our intuition, and that often causes us to 'go against the grain.'

When I was first pregnant, I was following all the rules until they started to feel weird to me. I was going to the doctor for my regular prenatal visits. I was curious and excited to learn all the things I needed to know about pregnancy, childbirth, and motherhood. My dreams were finally coming true.

However, those initial doctor's appointments resulted in long waits in the waiting room and more waiting in the clinic room. When the doctor would finally come in, I got so excited to talk about all things 'baby' and she was gone before you could say 'ultrasound.' This became the typical visit. I might get to listen to the baby's heartbeat for maybe twelve seconds before she rushed off to the next appointment. I had waited my whole life to listen to that heartbeat. Being rushed through one of the most pinnacle moments of my life was crushing my spirit. Each appointment, I was left packing up to go home sad and disenchanted with the hospital experience.

At twenty weeks pregnant, I decided to look for other ways to learn. I was researching nonstop on the internet and scouring all the pregnancy sites and forums to glean as much as I could about pregnancy, childbirth, and motherhood. When I found out that home births were still a thing, I became so excited. I immediately felt like giving birth at home was something I wanted to do.

I didn't even know what a midwife was until I did this research but I found a local woman in my area and she had availability for my due date. It was amazing. Everything seemed to be lining up for us. My favorite part about this new decision was that her prenatal visits lasted an hour or more. I got to listen to the baby's heartbeat as long as I wanted. I got to cry tears of joy with her. I got to share all my thoughts, feelings, and excitement with her. I knew this was the route I wanted to go. I felt sure that I could do it. I believe we as women were made for this.

During my visits, my midwife taught me what a doula was. I was shocked at the level of support that was available for childbirth that I had never been introduced to. At around thirty weeks pregnant, I signed up for a local doula's childbirth classes and hired her on the spot. I was so pumped to have options.

If you are thinking I've lived under a rock because I didn't know what midwives and doulas were, I felt that way as I learned more… but that is exactly my point. Historically, we have not been given a lot of options in life. Even in the Western world, where we have some of the most freedoms, we are not exactly taught what is in our best interest or best for our health. There are rules, norms, and standard practices that we are taught to blindly follow. It was by questioning and researching that I found more aligned answers and lifestyles for myself and my family.

Because we knew that we were going outside of the norm, this was something we kept quiet. We knew that our families would not fully support us in this decision. Having a home birth was 'out there' kind of thinking for our small Midwestern town. We weren't interested in any unsolicited feedback, advice, and fears, followed by long, drawn-out opinions about why it was a bad idea. So, we kept it to ourselves, and it allowed me to enjoy my plans in peace.

We knew what we wanted, and I was feeling so excited and empowered when, at thirty-three weeks pregnant, I went to the hospital with a partial placental abruption. I had to stay on bed rest for a week. I was diagnosed with preeclampsia and doctors prepared me for the worst. I was forced to consider an early labor because my blood pressure spiked to an alarming number.

The doctors knew I really wanted to deliver naturally so they offered to turn her from her breech position and then induce me. I made a split-second decision that I didn't want to put this baby through any more trauma. I didn't want to risk any more complications. After all that joy, dreaming, and planning, I had to come to terms with the fact that a home birth, and now natural birth, wasn't in the cards for me. At thirty-four and a half weeks, I made my first maternal instinct decision and delivered my baby via c-section.

I had finally found an aligned option, made all these plans and changes, and everything was abruptly taken out of my hands. It was all so traumatic, for me and my body. It was sad and overwhelming because once she was born, a month and a half early, I didn't get to see her for another twenty-four hours. She was whisked away to the NICU and put in an incubator all alone. I was wheeled to my dark hospital room to recover. It was happening so fast and so slow, all at the same time. After another week of NICU we were able to go home after seventeen days.

Things not turning out as planned is not always easy to talk about. It's a simple enough concept to comprehend, but not as easy to accept. Falling short of our expectations on a project, a dream, a vision, a relationship, or anything can leave us with a range of emotions to manage. We intellectually understand that we will probably have one or two experiences…more like one or two hundred let downs in our lifetime, but that doesn't make it any more tolerable to walk through the flames of disappointment.

There's pain, embarrassment, shame, guilt, doubt, insecurity, and more. Something we don't always acknowledge during these times of upset is grief. There is loss that we must face and process. There is potential loss in just about every situation, but the risk feels greater when you actively go against the grain. When you decide to go out on a limb and break rules to follow your desires or intuition, you are taking on a layer of risk that comes with an "I told you so."

Whether that is someone else taunting you or your inner critic nagging away, the loss in risk taking can have a little extra sting. What's important about this is that it doesn't really make the situation any worse. In fact, you tried something courageous and simply didn't hit the mark. A fact about any disappointment is that there is a lesson in it.

If you can change up your mindset and see disappointments for the lessons learned, you will be one step closer to success in whatever success looks like to you. Sometimes the setback isn't really a 'failure' but the closing of a chapter in your life that you are choosing to walk away from. Sometimes it's walking away from something that was no longer serving you to bloom brighter in another direction. As I shared in the last chapter, so often we are more present to the loss than the potential gain but consider that a perceived failure is simply a milestone toward your ultimate victory.

My second pregnancy went very much like my first. I had high hopes of a home birth, had preeclampsia again, was forced to accept a c-section, and left to grieve the loss of my dream. What made each situation bearable was that Noah was right there for us the whole time. He was splitting his hospital time between me and the babies and running home to keep our homebuilding business going. I felt so lucky that we had built a life working for ourselves that allowed my husband to be there for me when I needed him the most.

Breaking the standard rule to have 'secure jobs' secured our time and financial freedom. We have created jobs where we *can* take time off. I was able to say that I could retire by the age of thirty-seven. Heck, I could do the same for my husband if he ever wanted to quit working.

This wasn't a coincidence, accident, or fluke. It took years of clarity, focus, resilience, and dedication. It was that wild willingness to write and follow our own rulebook. Sure, we have encountered disappointments a few hundred times, but we have succeeded a few million times, and I will take that bet any day.

To sum this chapter up, which rules you break or follow is entirely up to you. This lesson isn't really about rules. It's about intuition.

Your gut instinct will always be your best guide in life, but it takes a certain skill set to be able to sense and follow your intuition. This lesson comes after the last chapter because having a clear connection with your inner authority is a result of healing, clearing, shedding, and releasing the gunk of your past. You have natural reactions that you may think are your intuition that are really your survival instinct driving your decision making. Those are not the same and you won't be able to distinguish which is which until you clear your head and heart of all the pain and trauma you have stored within.

So this is another public service announcement to begin your healing journey. Over time, this will continue to give you a better sense of yourself and what's good for you. It will also reveal a more authentic version of you that will step up as the true leader of your life. That you already exists within; what we are setting out to do is unleash it. That is exactly what we will be doing in the upcoming portion of this book. Buckle up, we are about to pick up speed.

Chapter 15

Breaking My Body

*"Massive wealth and abundance are
out there ready for you to claim as your own."*

Massive wealth and abundance are out there ready for you to claim as your own. I have proven that as I've created a multimillion-dollar company from scratch. However, I have learned that you cannot become truly free, financially or otherwise, until you've healed wounds that have been yearning to be healed. You can create all the money you want but if you are still broken inside none of that matters.

Throughout part three, I've shared how I've broken the mold, broken the bank, and broken the rules, and now I'm going to share how I also broke myself in the process. This part of the process was stuffed down with painkillers, caffeine, surgeries, and fueled by high octane pure adrenaline while I was working to break the cycles of abuse and hardship to build a life I loved. I wanted a life filled with stories of love and a legacy that could be passed on for generations.

What I have yet to explain is the severe and chronic health issues that I endured during most of my life and how they directly correlated with what was happening at those times. Asthma started at age five, coincidentally that was the same time that I started noticing my parents' abusive behaviors. My back pain issues started in high school around the same time I started bucking my parents' use of control, guilt, and manipulation tactics. You know about my pre-eclampsia issues during the births of both my children. This happened at the same timeframe I decided to stand my ground and cut ties with my father.

I'd gone back and forth several times in a relationship with my parents deciding whether to stop talking to them for a week, a month, or indefinitely. In an abuse situation, victims go back to their abusers several times before leaving for good. It is not an easy decision to make. I was motivated to get out of the mess I was born into because of the years I spent feeling held hostage in my own life.

The culmination of my tenure living under my parents' roof finally ended at age twenty-four when I had moved 'home' after my first year of teaching. I had just started working for a non-profit agriculture organization. The job expected me to move closer to the six-county territory that I oversaw, but I was renting a cute house two hours away, where I had been teaching that previous year. After much deliberation and a lot of driving, I knew that moving back in with my dad was the most convenient option because our farm was so centrally located for my territory. I wasn't ready to let go of my rental house just yet and rent was cheap so I kept paying for it. There was also a part of me that didn't want to give up that lease in case things didn't go well living at home.

I felt hesitant about the move because my parents were in the heat of the court battles over their divorce when I headed back to the farm to live with my dad. It was a work-from-home situation with many night meetings that I traveled all around for. I set up a small desk in my childhood bedroom with my company computer and printer. Because of the poor reception in the valley of our farm, when I got a phone call, I had to sprint all the way downstairs and outside to stand on one rock on the hillside so I wouldn't drop the call.

Since I was working from his home, my dad took it upon himself every day to sit on my bed and cry about how awful my mom was for leaving him. He was in the middle of divorce proceedings, which I tried my best to stay out of, but I had no escape. I knew he still had a temper just under the surface, so I tiptoed around any of my responses. I was really tired of being my parents' unofficial therapist but would casually remind him of his extremely poor behavior and their mismatched personalities as to why it was blatantly obvious that Mom left. He still never felt like he did anything wrong.

Within less than six months of this living and working situation, my dad and I ended up in a rage-filled argument. He was feeling upset about my mom leaving and there I was, again, reminding him of his poor behavior. He couldn't handle me calling him out for his temper, so his temper turned on me.

He chased me up the stairs to my room. I had made it in time to lock my door and hide under my bed and I laid on the floor quivering uncontrollably just praying to God that the flimsy hollow core door would hold up against his blows. It already had so many dents and dings in it. All the doors in the house did. This was nothing new. I held my breath and closed my eyes, willing the door to stand strong and stay shut. That door had held up in several arguments before, and luckily it held up for me once again.

Eventually, he gave up and went back downstairs. I heard the front door slam as he went outside and down to the barns. I laid there trying to collect myself and calm down. I knew that I had to get out. I knew that this was the end. I knew there was no coming back to this home again.

Luckily, for the first time in my life, I had a place to go. I still had my rental house. I was so grateful I had kept up those rental payments and had the foresight to do so. There was a part of me that hated how predictable he was and that I knew I would have to escape the situation, but being right didn't matter in that moment. Getting myself to safety was the priority. I climbed out from under my bed and packed up all my things as quickly as I could.

I kept looking over my shoulder to see if my dad was anywhere around to notice me shoving all my belongings into my company car. I knew he was at the shop or barn, but I had no idea for how long and I held my breath the entire time. His rage was always so unpredictable, and I couldn't get out of there quickly enough. I was gone within the hour.

I was so grateful that I had a safe place waiting for me to run to. I was relieved that I had finally made it to the point in my life where I didn't have to stay under that roof and suffer any longer. I *could* get away. I could leave. I had a choice. I was on my own. I was making my own money. I was free from that agony and after that day, I swore I would never be in that position again.

All these traumatic moments in my life showed me that it was possible for me to run from them, but that it wouldn't solve them. I became determined to build a life of wealth and security so that no one could control or manipulate me, but I had no idea that the trauma would get lodged in my body until I did the work to heal the damage and release it. Traumatic moment after traumatic moment getting lodged in your body starts to add up. When I first set my sights on financial freedom, I didn't know that our bodies could store trauma in that way.

If the traumas aren't addressed and healed, they create dis-ease in your body. This is where I believe much of my chronic pain comes from. Even to this day, I know that when my body starts expressing pain, it is a call for me to look inward. It is an opportunity to heal something that has previously gone ignored or unidentified. I was so grateful to have gotten out of that situation to start my own life and business. Yes, I eventually came to a place where my family had reached 'financial freedom,' but that wasn't the true solution. I wasn't truly free yet.

I thought we were all set. I had finally made it, and from that point on, I could just enjoy life. However, ease and joy were not the next steps for me. I had a lot more work to do and it was not in business growth. It was healing. Soon after reaching the point of thinking, *I've made it,* my body broke.

My body asked for deeper levels of healing, processing, and rest. It has been through so much in this lifetime. It has brought me so far. It had carried me out of the flames of abuse. It had carried two babies and kept us all alive when it was burning up with pressure. My body carried me through the hustling to build up our business to a place of financial safety and security, and it was spent. It was broken.

At many points of my journey, I was in so much pain I could hardly move. I could barely wiggle my toes without sending shooting pains up my back. I would get up and attempt to walk around my kitchen island holding onto everything I could grasp just to stay upright. I realized that if I didn't take better care of myself, I would need a walker just to get around before age forty. I planned to be retired and on fire at this time, dancing and singing, not inching out of bed in excruciating pain. I thought this period of my life would bring me freedom and all that comes with it. Especially as an advocate of daily exercise, that's not how I envisioned my freedom phase.

Over the course of my life, I visited many doctors, surgeons, and other professionals who said that there was nothing they could do for me other than to prescribe heavy duty painkillers and sign me up for more surgery. I knew I didn't want that anymore. I knew that was just a temporary patch-up job for a problem that required a real solution.

During visits with the many holistic health practitioners, acupuncturists, massage therapists, and more, I was told that I had been working at superwoman-like capacity for such a long time with little to no rest that my body was in a mode of self-preservation. It was rebelling against all action. My body was self-destructing, unintentionally, to protect me from myself. I knew that rest and healing was what was needed, rest above all else. If I didn't make changes in my life and take swift action to clear out my calendar to rest, I wouldn't have a life to enjoy.

Healing trauma is something I never thought would take that much effort. I underestimated the work when I thought I could out-work it. I didn't realize how literally traumatic trauma is to your body, mind, and spirit. I followed all the inspirational thought leaders, read their books, took classes, took action, followed through, started businesses, grew businesses, yet I didn't take into account the rest and recovery time needed after a 'max out.'

If you know about strength training, the rest and recovery period is often much longer than the max out session. I was taught that in athletics but not in life. I did not apply this understanding to my original beliefs about success. Society didn't teach me about rest and recovery either. Hustle culture is burnout culture. The high-level motivational speakers don't really talk about rest and recovery. I have yet to hear the high-achieving brand motivational speakers talking about how much time it can take to rest and recover from abuse trauma or max out trauma. Release work and inner healing wasn't talked about on those high-octane stages. They pump you up to go, go, go but don't tell you what to do when you've gone too far.

Recovering from abuse and trauma is a very specific and unique kind of healing and it is simply a step you cannot skip. I don't think we hear enough about it because it is more frequently talked about behind a new set of closed doors; closed doors to rooms that are safe to be in with professionals ready to handle the depth of work necessary to go to new heights of lasting health and wealth.

That said, I have a little confession. This book did not go as planned. When I first dreamt of my debut book, I imagined sharing all my real estate gold nuggets and teaching you all the ABC's and 123's of financial freedom. I wanted to bust out of the gate talking about investments, financial statements, saving, and spending. In the very early days when thinking of writing a book, I almost had that motivational speaker approach; *Go, go, go! Get, get, get!* I had been so successful that I thought teaching you to be successful had to do with where you put your money, but I had an important realization while putting this masterpiece together.

I realized why most people are broke. I knew this deep down, but I underestimated the importance of the lesson and how much it would take over the final product these pages turned out to be. You see, most people, especially most people picking up self-help books have some sort of vision and drive. You don't lack dreams or desire. You even know most of the steps to get most of what you want out of life.

While writing this book, I remembered that most people are broke because of the emotional baggage they are dragging around from their past.

Every new level of success and revenue surfaced wounds in me that I had previously been able to suppress and avoid. At some point, you will find yourself at a fork in the road: heal and clear the gunk of your past to become more successful or give up your progress and stay moderately comfortable where you are because you refuse to face your trauma.

So while I started this book *really* ambitious to step up as Becky the Dream Builder I was slightly disappointed when I felt more like Becky the grim reaper. I didn't plan on sharing all my traumas and dramas. I set out to write this book and, in the end, this book wrote me. It surfaced more than I felt ready to share, and I, sometimes reluctantly, answered the call because this book isn't about me. It is about you. It is about us. It is about our collective success and not just by becoming millionaire world changers. It is about truly breaking the generational poverty that isn't about money.

This book, because there will be more, became about healing our hearts, learning compassion, and coming together to drop the weight of our pasts. It's about being the hero we needed in our childhood and young adult years. Heck, maybe it's about becoming someone we needed yesterday but you can't become that someone if you aren't willing to face the pain you've run from forever. All the money in the world won't fill the hole in your heart.

I can only say that because there have been plenty of points in my life when the money we were making wasn't 'worth it.' I may have been earning to prove myself, spite someone, or ensure my independence and that almost always led to burnout. So, I want to make it abundantly clear that part of being broke is having a broken spirit. This doesn't mean anything bad about you or that you are wrong or unworthy. It means you, like every other person on the planet, have something to work on. Make healing your priority and good fortune will start flowing naturally.

Chapter 16

Breaking the Silence

"Reconciliation is a choice."

During the process of writing this book, there came a significant eighteen month pause between my perception of its completion and its actual fulfillment. Time and time again, I made finalization plans and repeatedly, those plans got pushed further out. There were days of frustration, confusion, and clarity throughout this process because it wasn't a logistical holdup. It was an energetic one. In retrospect, I can tell you that writing this book put me through a journey that I never imagined.

I acquired valuable lessons that with a premature publishing release, this book would have otherwise been incomplete without. It was only after the experience that I will share with you in this chapter that I finally understood the energetic delay. I came to understand that I was still in the process of arriving at a place of full circle healing.

To embody genuine peace, forgiveness becomes an essential requirement.

Though I had engaged in forgiveness exercises previously, I merely went through the motions until I reached a point of true readiness. You see, we can get through a lot of layers of healing before granting deep, freedom-giving, life-restoring forgiveness and it is not something that can be forced. It takes time, intention, and willingness to arrive at this place of inner harmony.

For many years, I clung to a multitude of anger, bitterness, and resentment, allowing these feelings to permeate my life. I thought I had forgiven before but I still held on to what made me so angry and it had become constrictive in my life. However, everything changed when someone posed two profound questions to me:

"How would I feel if my parents passed away without having forgiven or reconciled with them?"
"If I knew I had only twenty-four hours left on this Earth, how would I choose to spend that time?"

The impact of those questions took me by surprise. I remember going inward immediately and they rang throughout my mind, heart, and body for days. I really, deeply considered the end of my life. I considered a lot of other scenarios too and it brought so much to light for me very rapidly.

So after seven years of silence, I realized that I wanted my children to meet my dad and for him to meet them. This was one of the biggest decisions I have ever made. I have lived so intentionally to protect my family and to break traumatic cycles and before I reached the readiness level of forgiveness, I was unwilling to subject my family to the experience I had grown up in.

But deep down, I longed for reconciliation. And even deeper down, I still harbored love for that man. I genuinely desired change within our family with every fiber of my being. For the first time in my whole life, I really felt like there was an opportunity to create something new.

Eighteen months into writing this book, I made my first phone call to my dad in seven years.

I never planned for this specific day because for so long I felt I had made a final decision to keep him out of my life, so when I picked up the phone to call him, the phone seemed as big and heavy as a brick. I stared at my phone for three hours before calling him.

Earlier that week, I had a call with my coach to let him know that I was going to call my dad. He told me he was cheering me on and was proud of me for making that decision. He reminded me that to do this is an act of Christ; a Godly act. It is an act of divine intention. I felt so aligned making this move and I knew in my heart that it was time.

Even with all the clarity and encouragement I needed, the thought of actually making the call left me staring at my phone for hours. It was like the world around me didn't exist as I looked up his number. His contact 'Dad's Cell' was still saved in my phone somehow. I hadn't seen that name on my screen for years.

My heart sank and my hands got shaky but I knew I was ready. I pressed the call button. I felt my cheeks flush, my chest get hotter, and my breath get shorter with each ring.

On the third ring, he answered.

I gathered my breath and composure after I heard his voice for the first time in a long time.

"Hi Dad,…it's Becky. I think it is time for you to meet my kids."

"That sounds great," he said. "It's so nice to hear from you."

I finally exhaled when I could tell he was responding positively. "Maybe we could go to dinner," I proposed.

"I'll meet you anywhere, just let me know."

We decided on a burger and ice cream spot that my kids loved because I knew it would help them (me) feel at ease with the meeting. We agreed to meet the very next night at 5pm. Less than twenty-four hours later.

I could hardly sleep that night. I wasn't nervous but my whole body was buzzing with anticipation. There were so many unknown variables that I could not control or predict but I had already done year's worth of work to surrender to these feelings.

When we showed up, I knew exactly where my Dad was because he had brought a horse and wagon to give my children buggy rides, eager to show them who their grandpa was. They were so unaware and also elated. They did not know him from my point of view, only their precious, innocent perspectives and it gave me a new vantage point too. I was able to watch my children meet their grandpa and quickly grow fond of him. Over dinner, we had a wonderful, neutral conversation, catching up on the past seven years. It felt extraordinary. I felt extraordinary.

Subsequently, I also reached out to my mom, breaking a one and a half-year period of silence. We had a delightful, neutral Mother's Day lunch together, engaging in conversation and catching up. She expressed excitement at the prospect of seeing the kids again. It felt amazing to diffuse the tension that had existed between my parents and I. Each interaction was so liberating because they helped me release the anger, bitterness, and resentment that I had been holding on to.

Just one week after meeting with my dad, I received a call from his wife informing me that he had suffered a heart attack and was being airlifted to the local hospital. Without hesitation, I made my second call to my dad in seven years, and to my relief, he answered. He had just undergone surgery for a stent and was in recovery.

During that call, he said everything I had longed to hear.

He expressed how proud he was of me and how wonderful it was to meet my kids. He also acknowledged the greatness of my husband and I as a team. In his farmer wording, he told me that Noah and I worked together like a great team of draft horses who work side by side together, each depending on the strength of the other to get the job done. As a farm girl, I understood exactly what he meant by that and it brought tears to my eyes to hear him acknowledge the amazing team my husband and I have become; knowing he never had that kind of partnership with my mom.

I told him, "I love you," and he responded with the same words.

In that moment, an immense sense of peace washed over me. I felt the completion of a very long process. I recognized that what I experienced was full circle healing because I could feel a significant shift within me; one that felt like it changed me on a cellular level. We said our good-byes over the phone and a few days later, he returned home.

Now, this doesn't imply that things became some version of normal and we were suddenly one big happy family joining each other for Sunday meals. It means I changed from within. I discovered that I had placed unrealistic expectations on people, expecting them to be who I wanted them to be rather than accepting them for who they truly were. I had imposed my desires upon my parents.

I yearned for them to love each other and heal their marriage. I realized how I wanted that for them more than they did themselves. I wanted my mom to be the kind of mother who would go shopping with me, enjoy coffee dates, and engage in deep conversations about life, but that wasn't her nature. I wished for my sister to be my best friend, with daily phone calls, shared clothes, and sisterly discussions, yet that wasn't her inclination. I wanted my dad to treat us better and I expected family traditions to live on and for us to all get along in healthy, functional ways.

I grieved for my parents' lack of the ideal marriage I envisioned and for all the other aspects I previously mentioned. I felt sorry for myself for not having the picture-perfect family. Despite being married to the love of my life, I would question my own lovability. I felt alone as I continuously encountered these emotional barriers.

With enough disappointment, I had to let go of these expectations. Repeated disappointment throughout my upbringing broke me down in many ways where I took on protecting myself. I had put up walls and boundaries to protect myself but being asked those life-altering questions shook the foundation I so firmly stood on.

Finally meeting with my family shed a new light of possibility on my life.

Because of my jaded memories, I was not making room for who my people truly are. I was imposing upon them who I wanted them to be and the inner work I have done has shown me that if I want to be accepted for who I am, then I get to accept other people for who they are.

Just because I saw they weren't who I wanted or needed them to be didn't mean giving up. Rather, it meant creating space within our relationships so that I could heal and become aware of the unrealistic expectations I had placed upon these situations. I had to examine myself and learn my needs. I also had to truly surrender to who my people are without my impositions and a part of this process included a profound grieving period. I allowed myself time to mourn the loss of what I had desperately desired.

People sometimes make grief bad or wrong but I found that fully grieving was in fact the most healing part of my journey. It allowed me to fully acknowledge the loss I felt and to honor my wounds. This made true healing and forgiveness available.

Through my own healing journey, I have learned to heal my children and family. I am cognizant of the powerful connection between a mother and her children. I have discovered how to channel divinity into my being. I know how to employ meditation and prayer as vehicles for self-healing and the healing of my children, and all of these feel like superpowers.

The awareness I possess nowadays is something I wish I had attained decades ago, and I share it with you now, hoping you will find your own self-awareness much sooner than I did. I am grateful for the somewhat mysterious eighteen month period of obstacles that 'delayed' the timeline of this book's completion because it wasn't a timeline issue. It was a limitation in my perspective of what was needed to complete this book for the highest good of all.

As a result of that season of healing, retreating, and nourishing myself by surrounding myself with healers, coaches, and friends who supported my journey toward the level I aspired to reach, I can now see the tunnel I dug myself out of. I get to look back with a wholeness that is often hard to put into words. I gained this profound awareness at precisely the right time because now I have the privilege of sharing it with you.

If you are struggling with forgiveness, I want to leave you with a very direct message: Reconciliation is a choice.

Harboring bitterness, anger, and resentment is self-inflicted misery and you will realize that when you recognize that you have been clinging onto an imagined version of reality that may never come to pass. To hold on only brings you more pain and feelings of separation.

When you become willing to take an honest look within, you can forgive from a place of genuine peace; an ultimate treasure in this world.

When you embrace and embody a state of peace, no longer getting triggered or agitated by the same old scenes, then you have achieved true full circle healing. It feels akin to living in a meditative state, unbothered by the way people are. This also grants you access to the compassion you naturally have and want to share.

Through my healing journey, I have learned to accept people for who they truly are. I have regained the ability to enjoy life, embracing each day with joy. I have become comfortable with establishing healthy boundaries. I have learned to surrender to a state of allowing rather than striving for control. I have learned to observe rather than constantly interject. I have discovered the capacity to navigate through emotions and rise above them. I have mastered the art of release. I am now capable of sharing vulnerable messages with others without being overwhelmed and allowing those messages to stir up inner turmoil. All of this helps me live a life I am proud of and fulfilled by.

This is possible for you too, my friend. Let's continue on this journey together and I will continue to share how you can make it possible in your life. Perhaps you might be as well served by those questions I was asked:

"How would I feel if my parents passed away without having forgiven or reconciled with them?"

"If I knew I had only twenty-four hours left on this Earth, how would I choose to spend that time?"

I had to surrender the message that wanted to flow through my fingertips for the making of this book. It wasn't the book I 'wanted' but it was the book we all needed, me included. It became clear that I had a job to bring to light the garbage that holds us back without our knowing. It is the sticky stuff that operates in the background of our lives. If you've been through trauma let this be your chance to make that change, take that stance, and let your story out. This is your sign that you can rest, you can take time to recover, seek help, seek out sunshine, and enjoy life.

Let this be your wake-up call toward a fuller life and brighter future. The next portion of this book will have some inspiring next steps toward financial freedom but don't rush past the first three portions that emphasize your mental, emotional, and spiritual well-being. There is a season for everything, and it's okay to have a season of rest so you can ensure you have many more seasons of life to enjoy after that.

To be particularly responsible with my teachings, as we proceed into the last portion of this book you will really have to look within to decide *why* you crave and desire financial freedom. Earning all the money in the world won't change where you come from, how you grew up, or the memories you have. More likely, money will reveal them so you can heal them. Believe me, I have failed at out-earning my memory. No amount of money can change the fact that my past makes me sad sometimes. I have learned to accept my life as it has gone and look forward to a brighter future.

That said, we have arrived at the section I have been scratching and clawing to get to: the money section! I now know for sure that we have done the depth of work to get to a mindful conversation about money and I am so happy to have arrived here together. I am doing a happy dance over this computer as we head into talking much more about money and aligned action, baby! I hope you are as excited as I am. Feel free to do the happy dance with me as you take a stretch and a reset. See you on the next page.

Chapter 17

Breaking the Bank

"In real life, no one asks for your GPA or transcripts."

In real life, no one asks for your GPA or transcripts. Being a good student or having a certain degree is not the end-all, be-all of your success. In fact, if you poll ten people you know, I would bet nine of them aren't using their degree. At jobs, they ask for experience and references. For loans and big purchases, you will be asked for your financial statement and credit score. Being a good student won't get you any further than being a good financial planner.

If you are claiming that you want financial freedom, the first thing we are going to have to do is establish your definition of it. A few prompts to answer that question for yourself are located in the financial goals section on the next page.

Financial Goals

Let's talk about some money goals you have for your life.

Answer the following questions below:

• How much money is enough?

• How much money is too much? (Yes, you have a threshold for too much or you wouldn't be where you are right now.)

• How much money would set me free?

• What does being free even mean to me?

• What would I be doing if money were no issue? - No, really, when you are done sippin' piña coladas on the beach after three weeks and you get bored, what will you want to do with your time and life?

Those are some good prompts for now and I will have a few more as time goes on. To help you get a better understanding for goal-setting purposes, I want to share my definition of financial freedom: when your passive income matches and exceeds your cost of living.

Passive income is exactly that, passive. I like to call it 'the money you make in your sleep.' This is money that comes in around the clock whether you physically 'go to work' that day or not. This is not an employee type of income. This is not an hourly wage type income. This is an income stream where your money works for you.

Examples of this kind of money are: rental income from real estate investments, stock dividends, royalties, etc. Have you noticed that those types of income streams were not taught in school? Yeah, me too.

For different reasons at different stages of my life, I have found it frustrating that financial concepts such as passive income, investing, and credit are not taught in our formative years, or even insurance, taxes, and other administrative life responsibilities.

We were not taught in school how to be successful with money. I believe there are a lot of causes which we will not get into, but I want to point out a concept that you might not be aware you already understand. Talking specifically about it may point out some new levels of awareness and choice for you.

When and where I grew up, we considered ourselves hard-working people, who traded labor for a living wage. However, it was usually a measly living compared to the people who owned large investments or businesses, drove brand new Cadillacs, and owned vacation homes in far off places. This certainly isn't true across the board. There are some hard-working employees making substantial amounts of money, but for the intent of teaching the concept here, I am going to distinguish an important difference between a rich and poor mindset; or abundance vs. scarcity mindset.

Some will say it is a difference in social class and in some ways, it is, but another way to look at it is those with a poor mindset buy goods that depreciate when they get their hands on some money.

These are products and services that do not pay for themselves whereas those with a rich mindset *invest* their money into cash flow producing assets. These would be goods and services that do appreciate. In other words, they pay themselves off with extra income to spare.

Abundance-minded people are focused on creating long-term or legacy wealth and have their money work for them. Their consistent monthly cash flow and asset appreciation allows them to have the life they want to live non-reliant upon how many hours or days they work. The types of income and the ways they are spent are the very subtle differences that many people don't understand when from the outside looking in, it always seems like the *rich get richer* and they seem to be spending lavishly. Again, this isn't true across the board, but we are referencing the concept in theory, not in practice.

Since Noah and I have been together, we have had a very similar mindset on how money is spent. I think it is a major part of why we do so well together. We generally don't spend money on things that don't pay for themselves.

At times we've taken it to the extreme. Gift giving is a fairly non-existent love language for Noah. He has always been very frugal with money. For instance, Noah despises buying flowers on Valentine's Day and will instead buy them the day after for seventy percent off, if he buys me any at all. The same goes for Christmas presents. In fact, after a while, I just started buying my own, setting them out for him to wrap, and putting them under the tree so our kids could see Dad giving Mom gifts at Christmastime.

I certainly have had my scarcity mindset of drastically overspending or underspending. It all lived inside of a belief of lacking. I had my days of buying items I shouldn't have and going to dinners that cost me a month's worth of groceries. Those weren't wise spending habits and they cost me my peace and financial freedom. Scarcity in any extreme can cost you your personal and financial peace so it is important to strike a balance.

When we started our business together, we both agreed that we would rather reinvest our profits back into our business to double our profits. When we started this, I was still in a lack mindset so although we were starting to make more money, I was so programmed to be scarce that I felt broke. That's what landed me on old Trusty Rusty. Year after year, we kept reinvesting, and eventually, the passive income from our investments surpassed the amount of money needed to pay our bills. That, my friend, is financial freedom. In the long run, our plan paid off, but if I could have adjusted my perspective, I may not have struggled emotionally with the process as much.

We knew our long-term goal and stuck to it whenever we might have felt tempted to spend money that was meant to be used for the greater plan. This is something I will reference as your *why*. It is a driving reason and force in your attempts to persist with an overarching life goal. Throughout the rest of the book when I say *your why* or *my why*, I am asking you to consider the long-term vision for your life as opposed to an instant gratification, desire type of motivator. I say that because desire is sneaky. It will have you chasing the illusion of happiness in materials, achievements, or destinations and you will exhaust yourself and your bank account trying to reach fulfillment in those things.

We could have easily gotten distracted by the money we were making and the new spending power we had acquired. We were careful about how we spent both our time and money because we were so focused on financial freedom. Sure, there were years of dedication and sacrifice and a lot of risk-taking that many others don't practice but many others don't have the option to retire before the age of forty like we did.

I want to be super clear that the following paragraph is not a dig at individuals who are in a situation in which they are living paycheck to paycheck; I used to be like that. These 'rich' and 'poor' labels are used in this book to describe spending habits, not degrade people. Having a wealth mindset, for example, means that you are more focused on a long-term outcome than instant gratification. The poor have a nearsightedness that causes them to spend in self-gratifying ways that cost them more in the long run. They have to work longer and sometimes their minds and bodies can't work as long as they need to stay afloat financially. I have seen it time and time again and this can be very stressful for the person and their family. They become trapped in a paycheck-to-paycheck lifestyle just trying to keep up with bills and never have a breather to enjoy life. In fact, this leads to that 'I need a vacation' obsession when if they could develop better spending, saving, and investing habits, they wouldn't have a life they always need a vacation from.

I say all of this with love and the deepest commitment to impact. Awareness means everything. I used to spend beyond my means but I have learned the way to long-term wealth is not by living paycheck to paycheck. Having money was new and exciting and I was so disappointed to realize that the amount of money coming in from my paycheck barely covered my living expenses as a young single person. I couldn't imagine how I would be able to support the long list of other dreams I had for my life with just enough money to cover rent, groceries and gas. I didn't even know there were other options when I was young. I am sharing all of this so that you have new levels of awareness and choices. I want to help as many people as possible to break a cycle they may not realize they are caught in.

The major difference in this scarcity vs abundance concept and lesson is that the majority of people work tirelessly for their money. Those with a wealth mindset make their money work for them. I hope to impart the awareness that if you want to be financially free, you are going to have to adjust how you think money is made and spent. You will have to quite literally reprogram your brain away from the idea of trading your hours for dollars.

This next statement will apply on a person-to-person basis, but another thing you might have to reprogram is your perception of the wealthy. I think on a societal level, we have been made to believe that wealthy folks are all rich white men who are undercover criminals using the system to oppress the poor and keep all the money to themselves. That is not true. There may be people like that, but in general the wealth mindset is not that.

In this specific rich and poor analogy, I am offering that if you say you want financial freedom you are going to have to consider how money really works and work it. Strictly saving all your money is not the answer either. If you put a thousand dollars under your bed, its value will be less than a thousand dollars a year from now due to inflation. Saving every dollar you earn without a growth mindset and plan will bring you minimal reward and very little freedom. Money doesn't do anything on its own. It's the owner that knows what to do with it who can create generational wealth that is disaster-proof, so you must learn more effective ways of earning, spending, and investing.

Just like more saving isn't the answer, more work isn't the answer either. You could never singularly 'work' enough hours to become a millionaire. You could over a lifetime but that wouldn't be ideal. In fact, I just did the math for you. There are 8,760 hours in a year. Working every single hour of the year, you would have to make $114 per hour to make a million that year. Let's say you work 40 hours a week so that gives you 2,080 hours to make those million dollars. You would need to make an hourly wage of $480 per hour.

I am all for grand possibilities, but if we plan to make as many people as possible financially free as quickly as they can, I am not just going to send anyone off with advice about getting a higher paying job or going for the promotion. Of course, more money is helpful, but to reach massive goals, you are going to have to learn how to bend the laws of time, money, and energy. *That* will make you financially free.

To practice the rich mindset, you will need to learn the art of duplication, multiplication, and leveraging. This is shifting from the transactional "I do this, you pay me" mentality to the exponential "I invest this, it gains value without my effort" approach. You will have to learn how money multiplies itself when applied properly. In a few pages, I am going to explain this using some examples of our real estate investments, but first, let's finish defining financial freedom.

The second half of my definition mentioned 'cost of living.' You're probably more familiar with that. Cost of living is when you tally the amount of money you spend each week, month, or year. These aren't just your monthly bills. To get a very realistic figure here, you should track large and small expenses. When taking a real look at financial freedom, I am guessing you want to be able to spend freely, not just plan for the bare bones budget.

So, if we are going to make a real difference in your financial future, I am going to invite you to calculate your true cost of living and the cost of living the life you'd like to live. This will look and feel like budgeting. I know how the idea of managing finances can make people's stomachs turn, but you came here for the gold and you're going to get it. I am going to teach you the real secret of money management, the secret that makes all that cringeworthy work worth it.

The secret: you cannot exceed your own expectations.

That's right, my friend. You cannot hit a goal that you do not set. You have a subconscious limit to how much money you are comfortable making or have sitting in your bank account and that is the highest you can earn or keep unless you do the real work of creating a new outcome. You can do all the hoping, wishing, and praying you want for a magical ten-thousand-dollar month or coveted hundred-thousand-dollar month but if you have no idea how much you really need for your cost of living, all those numbers and dreams are arbitrary. Making a million isn't as rewarding if you are also spending a million. Sure, it's a great feat but if you are still waking up out of your sleep, choked by the anxiety of your expenses, you are no further than you were making a couple thousand a month. You must know your numbers.

So that your upper lip doesn't start sweating, I will leave the cost-of-living chart at the bottom of this chapter. You can do it later, I will spend more of this chapter pep talking you into doing it, but you might already be thinking to yourself, "crap, I would have to make *a lot* of passive income to cover my cost of living and beyond." Please don't get dismayed.

This is where your goals come into play. Like I mentioned, Noah and I had a focus on financial freedom and early retirement. Nothing got to trump our goals. Our spending was always put up for evaluation in reference to our commitment. We would ask ourselves, "is *this thing we are considering spending money on* in alignment with our long-term goals?" Our answer to that question was the answer to spending that cash.

This deliberation is how we would determine when to save, spend, and invest. As I briefly mentioned before, investing is notably different than spending. Investing promises to yield a return. Often, that return is earned through appreciation on the asset invested in, and this is exactly how we became financially free.

I love money and I love real estate, but I care more deeply about the welfare and well-being of my fellow citizens struggling like I did in my twenties. I was so fortunate to alter my life. There are so many millions of people who struggle all the way to their deathbed. I don't think that we are doing *everything* we can to positively alter the trajectory of our population, but I want to be an integral part of the shift. Whether it be with you reading this book, my courses and mentorship, by speaking to dozens, hundreds, or thousands on stages, I want to support our growth and evolution.

To get us back on track, I want to shift into talking about how you can use real estate as a tool for multiplying your money, duplicating your efforts, and leveraging your time. In my opinion, real estate investing is the best and most sustainable way to make your money grow exponentially. There are many ways you can make money in this industry, and I will share some that we have mastered. You can start from the ground up or enter into the game with some serious cash to leverage and multiply. Either way, I find it to be a generally fair playing field if you are determined enough to learn the ropes.

We started by simply buying foreclosed homes that were in need of repair, repairing those items, and then selling them all fixed up and move-in ready. As I mentioned in a previous chapter, our first house required no money down, but it was also *the cat pee house*. We had to put some serious work in so keep in mind that all options come with some sort of investment whether it be money, time, effort, or other resources.

We started with that two-bedroom, one bathroom, eleven hundred square foot 1970's foreclosed home for $42,000. It was in a quaint rural town in south central Wisconsin and on the intersection of two main roads of the town. It was in a good location and location is key in real estate investing.

This small home needed to be cleared of all the junk inside. It needed new windows, new shingles, the chimney capped, and some of the bricks needed repair. The wood siding needed to be painted and hardwood floors refinished as well as new cabinets, counters, wall paint, and some updated tiling in the bathroom.

We invested $20,000 into it. We did some of the work ourselves and hired contractors to help as well. We hired out for roofing, chimney masonry, windows, plumbing updates, and wood floor refinishing as well as cabinetry and countertop installation.

In this particular example, we flipped it for ourselves. We lived there for a year and half after remodeling it. It was fun to enjoy the fruits of our labor but we were also ready to make our money back.

We bought the house for $42,000 and sold it for $95,000. We invested $20,000 into it and after paying commissions to our real estate agent, we made a little over $20,000. If you factor it in the eighteen months we stayed there, we actually got paid to live there. Not a bad setup for some newbies. We got a delicious taste of success and wanted more.

In the course of our careers, Noah and I have done about a dozen flip homes together. We got so good at flips that we actually completely renovated one before we even closed on the purchase of it. This is not recommended; however, we were risk-takers and wanted to get going on the project. I think at some points we just liked challenging ourselves in these crazy ways. It's fun to write about, but we were definitely taking risks.

Some fix and flips can sell almost immediately. We listed one for sale right after we officially bought it, got to work, and got an offer right away. We made $20,000 on the exchange in two weeks flat. Fix and flip renovations of properties are a great way to get started making cash.

This is where the poor vs. wealthy mentality makes its difference. We could have spent that cash celebrating on something expendable and in the long run, had nothing to show for it. That would keep us on a hamster wheel of buy, flip, sell, party. For the sake of our long-term game, we celebrated over lunch and put the rest of that money into our next investment. We took care of our investments and now our investments take care of us.

Another way to keep your investment paying out is fixing houses or buildings up to rent instead of to sell. Being a landlord changes the income stream from a few major paydays a year to a string of steady income checks per month. Kind of like winning the lottery, you can take the lump sum or monthly payments. It's more about preference. However, my friend, if you are starting to get excited about $20k paydays, remember that this type of income is taxed at the same rate as normal income. You will need to set aside a certain amount of the profit for taxes depending on the state you live in. You must do your research and set yourself up financially for tax time or your big dream will become your worst nightmare.

If you have no interest in the construction side of a flipper, another great way to get started in real estate investing is to buy small houses or duplexes that are already in great shape to rent out. You can buy rent ready properties that require less hands-on labor. Keep in mind, being a landlord has its situations that will require a handyman, but you don't have to be that guy. Making a call for service is just as easy and you can still rock in this business venture even if you need to hire out for services.

Additionally, if you need a place to live, you could also buy a duplex, rent out one half and live in the other half. I love this idea and I think it is a really great way to afford getting started. The money that you make from the rental side could theoretically help pay for your mortgage, taxes, and homeowner's insurance, so you would be paid to live there. You are also earning equity in the property by living there as it appreciates in value so when you sell it, you will make a profit.

One thought I imagine might be running through your head is, "Becky, I don't want to be a landlord and get calls about clogged toilets at midnight." Yes, there is the possibility of this happening, but this is more of a limiting belief and fear than a daily or even monthly reality. I can tell you from personal experience, in over a decade of owning rental properties, this has happened maybe one time ever. During times like that, we called a plumber to help solve the problem and didn't have to unclog a toilet by reaching our hands into an icky situation.

I will say that if the fear of one call of a clogged toilet in the middle of the night is going to hold you back from financial freedom, this is your invitation to close this book and drop the idea of setting sail with this idea altogether. It may not be a clogged toilet you're worried about, but if you quiver at the mere idea of a 'shitty' situation, you will get discouraged when your stocks plummet on a bad month, or you try to start a business and run into basically any obstacle.

However, if you are willing to shrug that off and say "That ain't no thang! No big deal, I got this. Toilet schmoilett," then you, my friend, are well on your way to already achieving financial freedom in real estate investing and beyond. I invite you to be willing to roll up your sleeves and get dirty. A great thing to keep in mind is that there are structures you can put in place and teams you can surround yourself with, so you aren't going on this path alone.

If you are really loving the idea of real estate and building your own business, you might also get a lot out of our Building Dreams podcast where we teach more about life, love, and real estate investing. We interview other leaders in the industry and share tips, tools, and insights for real estate success.

Your success in any vehicle you choose to drive toward your financial freedom will be determined by your why and your strength of character. You could float onto the shores of financial freedom on a makeshift raft of woven-together coconut shells for all I care, it will be your commitment that will get you across the choppy seas of life. This is why your *why* is so important. If you want financial freedom, it is not sufficient enough to just want it to attain material wealth. You will have to hone in on your true *why* to stay afloat on this journey.

Our why was strengthened during the 2020 pandemic. It was a year of crisis for the entire world and there were plenty of statistics that represented how many Americans didn't have even a month's worth of emergency savings stored away. Millions of people lost jobs, went hungry, became homeless, and lost everything.

2020 was also the year we became millionaires. The income from all of our businesses plus the equity gained in properties we had purchased was over one million dollars. When we learned this, Noah and I looked at each other, floored. We had reached our ten-year goal in the single most challenging year of the collective human race.

The good feelings that came with having financial security came at a time of major panic in the world. People were losing jobs, whole industries were being shut down overnight, and there were shortages left and right. We definitely celebrated ourselves and enjoyed the high of reaching such a phenomenal goal, but my heart ached for those struggling with the worst times of their lives in that year.

I flashed back to the Becky riding Trusty Rusty to her thirtieth birthday praying someone would buy her dinner. I thought of the Becky with medical bills larger than her annual income. I thought of all the parents who suddenly had to figure out homeschooling while trying to put food on the table and felt more driven than ever to get this information into the world, my way. The Becky way.

I speak up so much about the shortcomings of the education system because of years like 2020 making it glaringly obvious that we have not been taught the fundamental concepts of succeeding as adults. More people than ever before were forced on government assistance and the country faced the impact of inflation to match. There are waves of impact to any recession, and it is one of those 4 D's we are trying to protect ourselves from. Financial freedom and education are more essential than ever.

That is why I want to teach you exactly how to budget, save, and invest in a proactive way. So, without further ado, let's talk about your cost of living. You can do this, and I can promise you will be happy you did. Just don't quit halfway through. There is a breakthrough in finishing this exercise. Your future self thanks you.

So here, get out a notebook and write down all your monthly expenses. Below is a pretty thorough list of expenses to consider that ranges from needs to wants, and extras. There are always the obvious recurring bills but there are so many things we spend money on that never really get tracked. I added a few below to really take a look and find out exactly where your money is going.

Many people are actually making way more money than they realize but they are also spending recklessly and don't realize that either. A way to find these true numbers out is to open your banking app and acquire the last three months' worth of your bank statements with the lists of transactions. Then, get your trusty highlighter out and highlight all those times you go out to eat. Track those nights out. Look at how much gas you need and how many times you add a snickers bar when you go to pay at the counter.

I once had a client tell me that they didn't want to track their money because they weren't bringing in as much as they were spending so there was nothing to budget, but *that is* exactly the point. If we never create accountability around our spending, money will respond to us in a mirrored way. If you are careless with money, it will hardly come to you.

It is when you respect it, track it, invest it, care for it, and value it that it will respond in kind. It's finally time to change your story. It is time to change how it goes with you and money. It's time to make your money work for you.

Use this list on the Tracking Expenses work page and in a notebook, average your three-month spending on each item. Cross off what doesn't apply and add your unique expenses to your list. I promise, the outcome will tell you a story. It will reveal truths and options to you. It won't be all bad. There is much to learn here and reviewing your finances is a *real* first step towards *real* financial freedom.

 # Tracking Expenses

EXPENSE	MONTH 1	MONTH 2	MONTH 3
Mortgage/Rent	--------	--------	--------
Homeowners Insurance	--------	--------	--------
Property Tax	--------	--------	--------
Auto Insurance	--------	--------	--------
Health Insurance	--------	--------	--------
Medical Costs	--------	--------	--------
Life Insurance	--------	--------	--------
Utilities	--------	--------	--------
Water	--------	--------	--------
Sanitation/Garbage	--------	--------	--------
Groceries/Toiletries	--------	--------	--------
Car Payment	--------	--------	--------
Gasoline	--------	--------	--------
Public Transport	--------	--------	--------
Internet	--------	--------	--------
Cell Phone	--------	--------	--------
Student Loans	--------	--------	--------
Other Loans	--------	--------	--------
Child Care	--------	--------	--------
Clothing/Jewelry/Etc.	--------	--------	--------
Dining Out	--------	--------	--------
Alcohol/Cigarettes	--------	--------	--------
Movie/Event Tickets	--------	--------	--------
Gym Memberships	--------	--------	--------
Travel Expenses	--------	--------	--------
Streaming Services	--------	--------	--------
Monthly Subscriptions	--------	--------	--------
Self-Care	--------	--------	--------
Home Decor	--------	--------	--------
Emergency Fund	--------	--------	--------
401(k)	--------	--------	--------
Retirement	--------	--------	--------
Investments	--------	--------	--------
Credit Card Payments	--------	--------	--------
Taxes	--------	--------	--------
Registrations	--------	--------	--------
Renewals	--------	--------	--------
Donations	--------	--------	--------

Part 4

Chapter 18

The Shift

*"Everything that is currently happening in your life
is a result of the choices you have made."*

Well! How was your financial review session? I hope you did it and worked on it thoroughly because I have no doubt it was an insightful experience at the very least. The thing to remember is there is no quiz about it. I won't be checking in on you to make sure you did it. That exercise is for you, not for me. I offer it because it offers freedom.

There are a few twelve-step programs out there which describe that the first step of making a change is admitting you have a problem. If your disempowering spending habits only ever exist in the background of your life, they will silently and subtly run it. This is the reason many people can't really grasp why things aren't working out for them. You must observe your patterns, habits, and cycles to make any sort of substantial shift. So, if you worked on your expense tracking, wonderful. Great job. If you skipped that step, I encourage you to go back and work on it. If you feel resistance to this step, it is likely that there is healing to be done first.

There are no *wealthy* millionaires who don't know their numbers. There may be *rich* millionaires, who would be considered people with a poor mindset who happened to come upon a windfall of money and often lose it all. These are people who win the lottery, get an inheritance, or hit a jackpot of some sort. They get all excited about their new spending power and blow it as quickly as they got it. This also puts them deeper in the hole than when they started because they set themselves up with more expenses than they can afford to keep up with when the money runs out.

This is why if you don't start tracking and managing your money now, you can't truly be wealthy. You don't just decide to start budgeting when you have money. The habit, belief, or behavior comes first, the manifestation comes second. Money flows to stewards who will respect it and use it wisely. Money quickly flows away from those who abuse it or disrespect it.

Think about it this way, if money were a person, how would your relationship with that person be right now? Would Money want to stay in a relationship with you or leave you for the next person who gives it more love, care, and attention? Being intentional about your money will certainly bring more of it to you. Then, you will finally be able to live out your dreams of financial freedom.

In this last part of the book, I am inviting you into the wealth club: the portion of the population who make, keep, and multiply their money. You will become a part of an even more elite percentage of this group because I know you are someone who also wants to do good and make a positive impact with all that money you'll have.

In this chapter, we are going to talk about core shifts that must take place in your head, heart, and body to become a wealthy person.

Having a Growth Mindset

Something I realized in the process of creating a business that is now a well-oiled machine is that we have tested our breaking points. As in any business when you are testing out a new machine, a new medication, or a new product you want to find out where its breaking points are. You want to find the point of weakness of the product, machine, etc. This helps with the improvement process.

As a human testing out your breaking points, consider where and when you quit. When do you stop reaching for your goals and dreams? What stops you? What intimidates you into submission? Those are the breaking points you want to recognize so you can make a shift in those areas to continue evolving and improving. When you have an improvement mindset, you are constantly expanding toward your fullest potential.

Everything in life is a lesson. If we quit too soon, we have denied ourselves the breakthrough of learning the lesson of the breaking point. You can find nuggets of information every day if you are in that mindset. You learn to keep going and learn to make tweaks along the way.

This type of mindset requires you to be okay with challenges and feeling like you are breaking, but you must remember at these times that breakdowns lead to breakthroughs. This *is* the function of learning and evolving. If you stay the course, then soon enough, the learning happens faster and faster. You become more efficient, and you begin to experience yourself as more capable, powerful, and expansive. This will help you reach your full potential, but first, you must learn, recognize, and move past those breaking points. This is where your dream life resides.

Knowing When it's Time to Make a Change

How do you know when you know you are needing change? There have been multiple times in my life when I thought, *this is it! I love my life. I have my dream job. I'm going to be doing this forever,* only to find out within a few months that shifts were happening to change my trajectory; many of which I didn't see coming.

Often, you can tell you are in need of a change because you start having a visceral reaction to people, places, and situations. This means that your body starts communicating with you in feelings and sensations to get your attention. This happens on both ends of the spectrum. You will feel excitement, joy, and other good bodily feelings when something is aligned for you. When something is out of alignment, it feels uncomfortable, icky, weird, or downright painful. If you learn to listen to your body, you will know when you are in a situation that is out of alignment with your highest good and the highest good of all. This is often referred to as *body wisdom,* and you have it.

During the custom homebuilding portion of our lives, I would normally get all giddy and excited to see new construction homes going up; a vision manifesting right before my eyes; a new home for a family; so much promise and potential. I just loved what we were doing.

Once we had hit peak levels of success in our business and burn-out started to kick in, pulling up to a new home made me want to puke. I literally felt repulsion throughout my body. I pushed through it for a while, but it became impossible to outwork the feeling. One Monday, I felt nauseated all morning and for a few mornings after that. Something had shifted in me that I could no longer ignore.

I would get to the office and basically within thirty minutes of being there, I would start crying for no reason at all. Well, for no reason obvious to anyone else. Deep down, I knew the truth. I was done. I was done with what we were doing. I was done with being so stressed out. I was done with high client demands. We had taken on too much at once but that was just who we were back then. We didn't want to build three to ten custom homes per year like most builders of our size. We did it to ourselves, but I decided that I wasn't going to do this to myself any longer. I needed to be done. I needed to make a serious change.

The hard part when you are in business for yourself is that you can't just put in your two weeks' notice. You have to finish the responsibilities at hand. You have to complete the contracts you signed and fulfill the agreements you made. We trusted ourselves to finish the work we had started but we also decided to create an exit strategy. The simple act of acknowledging this shift felt much better and made finishing out our responsibilities much more manageable and physically tolerable.

The real shift was that we acknowledged the misalignment and committed to getting back into alignment. This kind of transition requires self-awareness and courage, and you have the potential for both.

Making a serious life change demands a level of self-responsibility that most people aren't willing to practice. It is usually easier to just stay small, safe, and comfortable. We often settle for our comfort rather than our success because we know what our comfort zone is like. The only time anyone really makes a change is when the discomfort of change outweighs the discomfort of staying the same. These are those exact times that your body communicates with those visceral reactions and ignoring the need to shift becomes literally and figuratively excruciating.

Everything that is currently happening in your life is a result of the choices you have made. Life happens, yes, but it is your reaction to what happens that dictates your personal outcomes and manifestations. You are not a victim in your own life. You have the power to make change.

There are millions of people who play victim in their own life and get stuck in their discomfort and unhappiness. This happens to people who complain and blame and it serves them no good. They may never see it this way because it is confronting to take such high levels of responsibility for one's life. You would have to admit that you have given your power away to your excuses or the people and situations that trigger you. If you really want to make a change, you will have to take responsibility for your life. The sooner you do, the faster you will head in the direction of living your dreams.

All in all, consider that you know when it is time to make a change; especially if you now recognize that you are having visceral reactions to your current situation. Sometimes it's nausea. Sometimes it's pain, sadness, fatigue, or generally feeling like crap. It can feel like lack of motivation or crippling anxiety or insomnia. Your body will do anything it can to communicate its need for change, but you must learn to listen to your body.

If you are having visceral reactions to your current living space, job, or relationship, that might mean it's time to listen to those body sensations. Listening to your body simply means acknowledging what you feel and shifting from despair and complaint about the pain to a genuine inquiry about it. What hurts? Why does it hurt? I often like to ask the pain, what are you trying to tell me? This might sound a bit mystical in the Western world but if you practice listening to your pain as if it were a message from your body, you might find guidance in it.

This can be big or small. You can simply rearrange or re-organize your space. Change your wardrobe, eating habits, or fitness routine. Become more intentional with your schedule and deprogram being busy all the time. It might become clear that you need to have a tough conversation you have been avoiding. You may decide to include new practices like meditation, journaling, and therapy, or coaching.

If you are feeling a stirring and general discomfort within, that very likely means the season of your life is changing. Your job is to shift with it. You wouldn't keep wearing your summer clothes when fall and winter hit. Change is a part of life. Embrace it and it will embrace you and bring all the blessings you pray for. It's time to take baby steps and map out how to make the change in the direction of your dreams.

Know Your Why

To map out your future, let's talk more about *why* you are here. I'm just going to go out on a limb and say you probably picked up this book because of its promises of inner peace and financial freedom. The knowledge and action steps around money are important, yes. Money management is essential, investing will make a difference, and understanding vehicles for success will all get you where you want to go, but we must talk about why you want it so badly.

I want you to take time after this chapter to journal about your why. Don't rush up to do the next thing after you are done reading but instead, take some extra time to sit in silence, drop into your heart space, really ponder the following questions, and listen for the answers from within.

Know Your Why

What is it about financial freedom that I want so badly?

When I think about financial freedom, what do I imagine and envision?

If I were already financially free, what would my life look like?

If I had already made it, what would I be thinking about now?

What will financial freedom provide me?

Finish the sentence: I desire financial freedom because it will…

If I have all the money I need and more, what would I do with all the overflow cash?

How do I look, walk, talk, and act as a financially free person?

If I am financially free right now, who does that make me?

Something that many people don't realize is that when you reach financial freedom and check off all the dream boxes, there will still be life left to live. It is an illusion to dream that once we have the proverbial *house on the mountain top* or whatever dream you envision, that you will be 'done,' and you can finally 'relax.' That is not true because life is not about achievements, accolades, or acquisitions. From every mountain top, you have the altitude to set your sights on a new mountain top. This perpetuates the cycle if you aren't rooted in your why.

If you want to be truly wealthy in a lasting way that won't demolish you along the path, you are going to need a more authentic force fueling the engine of your desire. Without a strong enough why, you will not make it. You will not go for the long haul. When the going gets tough, you will quit. No material goal of riches will be worth the emotional growth and stretching required of you to be wealthy.

You are completely allowed to want to manifest material representations of your abundance and success. Your personal desires are not to be ignored. Everyone has unique visions of their most abundant life, and we don't all want the same things. That is a good thing. It levels out the playing field. That's what makes life fun and interesting and that's what makes the world go 'round. If we all follow our unique passions, all the needs will be met by us aligning with our roles in the world. The same way animal species self-govern and survive, we could do so by fulfilling our God-given gifts and roles. I am simply encouraging you to consider your deeper core values that drive your willpower to show up for the task at hand.

You may have a gift or passion that you would love to get paid to do for the rest of your life. You may have an urge to help people in a certain way and make a living off of it. You might have a hobby that you would love to turn into a business or possess a very technical skill that the world needs. You might want to dedicate your life and work to a cause that inspires and excites you. You may see a gap in the market and the needs of humanity that can be solved with an invention or innovation.

These are root-centered whys that will keep you showing up for work that might challenge you from time to time. Personally, the idea of helping people heal from trauma and become free enough to thrive in life gets me out of bed every morning. The dream of teaching financial literacy and real estate wealth puts butterflies in my stomach and brings a smile to my face. Even building homes for families to grow in brought me a deep sense of satisfaction and contribution. Thinking of making enough money for our family to live happy, healthy, and well makes my heart burst with energy to show up for my whys and my work day in and day out. My whys push me beyond my physical limitations and my limiting beliefs. They have always helped me move past barriers that I feared would be the end of the road, but I have to keep those whys at the front of my mind when the load gets heavy.

You have your whys deep within you, and I am asking you to look past your instant gratification type of desires to look for your gifts and calling. When you afford yourself the awareness around your core values, you will be able to afford anything. Following your path will align you with people, places, opportunities, and resources that will fund your way and bridge the gap between you and your dream life. Also, keep in mind that money is not the only manifestation of wealth. Following your purpose and path will lay before you all the tools you need along your journey to financial freedom.

The Power of Your Language

To rise above where you currently are, you need to take an assessment of your daily beliefs, thoughts, words, and actions. Paying more attention to what comes out of your mouth on a regular basis is one of the fastest ways to change your life. You will find out very quickly if those beliefs, thoughts, words, and actions are keeping you where you are and what changes are necessary to get you where you want to go.

When I realized the power of our thoughts, words, and beliefs, our lives shifted from stagnant and depressing to alive and revived with rapid acceleration. Two popular adages for this lesson are: *change your thoughts, change your world and you attract what you put out into the world.* Keep those in mind while I tell this story.

I had first seen the movie, *The Secret* by Rhonda Byrne about the Law of Attraction back when we were living in our very first home. We were proud of that little home. It was the home that started our entire real estate investing career and our marriage. Life was perfect while it was but our dream was to live in the country, and that dream couldn't come soon enough. Our bedroom window in that house was only a few feet away from the public sidewalk and it was a feature neither of us liked or were used to.

We both grew up in the country and talked about moving back often, but that goal seemed further down the road. Our house had been up for sale for about eight months at that time but had very few showings and even less offers. We were starting to feel defeated. After a year and half of living there, one random night, Noah, who doesn't typically cry, fell to tears because he wanted so badly to be living in the country. He was having that visceral reaction we could no longer ignore.

I had just learned from that movie, *The Secret*, that if I changed my beliefs, thoughts, and words, and took inspired action that things would start falling into place for where we would be moving next. The very next day, I went down into our basement and started boxing up all of our belongings. When Noah came home that night, he asked me what I was doing.

I simply told him that we weren't going to live there anymore. We were going to find a place in the country, so I was boxing up our things and getting ready to move. I had absolutely no *real* idea how things were going to work out but I was more than willing to trust that they were.

I started boxing up our belongings and no more than a month later we found our dream fixer-upper farmstead in the country. Almost simultaneously, we received an offer on our home. Everything was falling right into place for us, and I knew it was because we had changed our attitudes, perspectives, and actions. Within two months we had moved out and had purchased the four-acre farmette.

The next lesson about positively shifting your beliefs, thoughts, words, and actions began immediately with the remodel of our new humble abode.

The house ended up being more of a dump than we had originally thought. The trusses were completely broken and barely holding up the roof. The majority of the framing needed to be completely replaced. We found horsehair stuffed into the plaster, lath holding the walls up, and walnuts hidden by squirrels who lived in the attic falling all over our heads as we pulled down pieces of the dropped ceiling.

We gutted the place piece by piece, crowbar pull by pull, and sledgehammer jab by jab. It was gross and it was hot; literally one of the hottest summers on record. It was dirty, dusty, sticky, and musty. It was starting to feel like a mistake and the heat wasn't helping my attitude. Suddenly, our little dream became a hot, sticky nightmare.

I was complaining nonstop as we worked on the place. As the demolition got worse, I would catch myself constantly announcing 'this sucks!' over and over. Eventually, I could tell it was also affecting everyone around me. My husband, his cousin, and friends were all helping gut the place and I could tell everyone was thinking what I was saying.

I could see the impact of my attitude and thought about the lesson we had just applied from *The Secret* two months before. I decided that I could shift my impact. I decided that repeating *this sucks* over and over was not going to make the situation any better or make any of us feel any better about the shitty process that it was.

So, I made an intentional shift and started saying, "This is so awesome! Isn't this just great?" Yes, I might have had a snarky grin on my face and been totally sarcastic at first but eventually, things changed in real life. We all started using more positive words to describe this less-than-ideal situation. Even if they may have been a bit sarcastic at first, the smiles that the joking brought to our faces were authentic and so was the laughter. Eventually, everyone started having more fun, and the place actually started coming together with speed and ease.

I have applied this lesson thousands of times now and it has made me millions over the years. You get to pick your reality by how you think and talk about it. *You* get to determine your outcomes by how you react to your current circumstances. It is up to you but you must have the awareness and self-responsibility to do so. The great news is that you can start today!

Gratitude

The fastest way to get the shift started today is with gratitude. A gratitude practice is one of the simplest, most natural ways to adjust your mindset and reality. It is the secret sauce to attracting more quickly.

So many people underestimate gratitude as a cheesy exercise your great-aunt recommends when she says, "Count your blessings, dear." However, I mean it wholeheartedly when I say, the more seriously you take on gratitude work, the more fully it will impact your life. The fun part about gratitude is how almost immediate the transition can be. You can instantly lift your spirits, perspective, and frequency to become a match for better outcomes and manifestations with the quick change of your thoughts, words, and actions.

Another thing to keep in mind is that you cannot hate and judge your way into abundance. If you make a change from hate, anger or resentment, you will manifest a similar experience to reteach the lesson until you learn it. Gratitude is a life lesson that will help you out of situations you would rather not be in. You must learn to find the blessings in every moment of every day, even when life doesn't look exactly as you planned.

In my example above, when I was hating and judging our farm remodel, it was miserable. When I decided to turn my attitude into gratitude, the 'fun switch' was flipped and the blessings poured in. It can happen so quickly if you are willing to get started swiftly.

Think about it, how often are you really counting your blessings and expressing your gratitude? Are you saying thank you when you wake up, and feel blessed for a new day? Are you grateful for the water you drink and the clothes you wear? What about the birds chirping, the sun shining, the sounds of your kids laughing, or a hug from a loved one. We get so used to so many of our luxuries that we forget that they are in fact luxuries and privileges. When we start to overlook them, we lose our sense of appreciation for the beautiful details of living.

One thing I can promise you is that if you can't be grateful for the little things you have now, the big successes will have very little sense of reward as well. The bliss of achievement will be temporary, and you will be plagued with always having to achieve more to feel that flash of happiness. That is an exhausting life to live. Gratitude for each detail of your life will make all things, big and small, the best thing that ever happened to you. You must stay present to your blessings to call more in. You can use this practice to do exactly that. Calling more in with gratitude is a wonderful way to manifest a shift in your life. Live as if today is the best day of your life, because it is. There will not be another today.

You can also feel gratitude for things you dream about having. This is called visualization, but it is rooted in a deep sense of gratitude and faith. You can say thank you for your dream car and envision sitting in the driver's seat. You can say thank you for the beautiful dream home you built before you built it. Practice imagining what it will feel like to cook breakfast and sip a cup of coffee in your new kitchen in the morning. Keep finding things to be grateful for that are in your current reality and also things you desire as if you already have them. The universe acts accordingly. This will lead to quick and drastic shifts.

Gratitude really makes my heart flutter because there is already so much beauty in our lives. I want to wrap up this segment by inviting you to simply take a deep breath and exhale the words *thank you.* Look around and notice the chair you are sitting on and the time you have to read this book. Find yourself grateful that your eyes work to read these words. I can tell you with certainty that I am grateful we are here together to make these positive shifts.

Keeping a Positive Outlook

Speaking of positive shifts, I want to teach you one of my super-powers. I believe that my sunny disposition has led to most of the shifts in my life. It has moved me down the path of progress day in and day out. Year after year, my positive, optimistic attitude has kept me winning in life. Sure, life has its challenges, but it is the way that I keep my chin up and eyes on the horizon that has successfully moved me through pain, challenge, and trauma. I am always willing to believe in a triumphant outcome and because of it, I triumph more often than I don't. I believe it to be one of my greatest assets and I hope to impart some of my sunshine onto you.

I've always had a very bouncy, positive, silver lining outlook on life. As far back as I have memory, I have felt this way. Despite all the trauma endured from watching my parents lashing it out for the majority of my life, I have kept this empowered attitude.

This positive approach to life has always led me to surround myself with positive people and situations. I attribute my sustained upbeat energy to having some amazing friends and support structures around me, especially when I needed them most. I believe that my life's challenges have only strengthened my optimism and solidified my purpose of shining my light and faith for others to follow out of their darkness, just like my supportive friends have for me.

I can fall off the bandwagon from time to time and I notice what happens around me when I do. Things fall apart, I get frustrated and short fused, and life starts to get messy. I have witnessed it enough times to recognize it and so can you. Watching for the manifestations of a bad attitude can signal you to make the shift.

Think about it from the outside looking in, take a mental note of people in your life who always speak negatively. Aren't their lives a pretty direct reflection of their negative talk? They constantly have to face struggles, breakdowns, and frustration. They are usually suffering from some offense, failure, and ailment. They may not have been taught how to turn it all around.

For starters, that was the intention of the whole first portion of this book, but after healing comes intentional transformation. Beware of not only the thoughts you think but the words you speak. When you speak, speak only of the things you want, speak of goodness, speak in the highest form. Speak of your success and triumph and there is no doubt in my mind that you will have it. What comes out of your mouth will come into your life. If you want to make waves in creating the life you've always wanted, the simplest thing you can start doing today is change the way you think and speak about your life.

The different aspects covered in this chapter are designed to have you consider the many facets of your success. Personal and financial freedom are no accident. They are a culmination of all the little details put into motion. Your body will tell you. Your awareness will teach you. Your why will drive you. Your gratitude will bless you and your attitude will progress you. Keep stepping forward in full faith that what you dream of is on its way to you.

Chapter 19

Let Your Mess Become Your Message

"We eventually reach an age where we realize no one else is responsible for us. Then we have to take a serious look in the mirror to meet ourselves about the pain we have actually caused ourselves."

The good Lord knows I was raised in a mess. There are plenty of times I have felt like a mess in life. Noah and I have made messes in business. I've been an emotional mess at times. Physically, my body was a mess that stumped medical professionals. Sometimes, my house is a mess like when our daughter rode our miniature horse into the kitchen, or our son took his diaper off in a raving rebellion.

I have felt messy at different times for different reasons, but I have always known that deep down, I am made of so much more. I am made of fire, passion, light, love, and joy. During any messy days, weeks, or months, I rely on that sunny disposition I mentioned in the last chapter. I trust myself to turn lemons into lemonade, every dang time.

In fact, many people who have heard my story wonder how I have been able to keep such a positive spirit and overcome the obstacles I have faced. I often get (deeply appreciated) sympathy for growing up in an abusive upbringing, but I am clear that is not *who* I am. My upbringing shaped a lot of how I turned out, but I have always been determined that my past will not define me. There is too much available and possible in this lifetime to write the rest of my story from the head and heart space of yesteryear.

I have chosen to share my story because I was shaped, carved, primed, and polished by the life I have lived. All the ups, downs, the hard left turns, and even the right hooks have helped me develop into the strong-willed, passionate woman that I know myself to be. I have had to heal and shed old identities, beliefs, and behaviors that would hold me back and keep me small, but I have learned to accept my life for how it has gone.

It wasn't always that way though. I have had such a positive attitude that most people didn't learn about my upbringing until my mid-thirties. I've always been so upbeat and generally joyful that people have been shocked to hear about the trauma I have endured. I used to stuff, compartmentalize, and avoid the darker side of my past. I used to try to shine light on it to make it seem less sad. Even when writing this book and telling tough story after tough story, I felt inclined to soften it up with a lighter memory. Trouble was, they were so heavily outweighed by the yelling and fighting. I had to learn to accept that and grieve the childhood I wished I had.

I had to accept the parents I had and give up trying to turn them into the parents I expected, needed, or wanted. I stopped trying to change them and learned to love them and leave them where they were in their journeys. Life takes us through phases, and I will always do what's in my heart and for my health, so I will rely on my intuition to guide me through my tough days in the future. I have learned enough from my own messes that the message I am sharing with you in this book was mine to follow first.

It has been a tremendous relief to tell my story because I can so clearly offer you the message that has emerged from the mess of turmoil, confusion, and pain. If you were to walk away from this book knowing just one thing, I would hope you would have learned that you can go through hard times and come out the other side triumphant.

You can go through abusive situations and still go on to create multimillion dollar companies, healthy marriages, and happy families.

You can choose better, stand your ground, and decide you're worth having a happy, successful life. What that's going to take is waking up from any victimhood you may be struggling with and starting to awaken the leader within you. You will need to stake a claim over your life, take your power back, and make choices about your future that excite you.

My friend, being a victim of your circumstances is not a fun place to be. It can make you sick, broke, angry, and tired. There is no need to be embarrassed about where you are or what you might be struggling with. There is help and hope out there.

There is a major stage in healing that must be acknowledged if we ever want to move forward in life: forgiveness.

First, there is the forgiveness of others. Like I mentioned, I had to release my parents from my expectations and resentments. You may have heard the adage that holding a grudge is like drinking poison and expecting the other person to die. Your anger and sadness will kill you if you never release the people you are upset with from the clutches of your emotional punishment.

I have seen people ruin their own lives to show their families, exes, or old bosses how badly they got screwed up from their past experiences. It serves as a *see, look what you did to me* type of statement, but it only really affects themselves. It proves nothing other than you are stuck in that memory, still under someone else's influence. I completely understand the pain another person can cause, and it is your responsibility to heal and thrive. The other person cannot thrive for you and there is no apology they can give you to truly fill the hole in your heart. You must fill that with your own identity, purpose, and destiny. You must rise up from the ashes of your heartache and fallen dreams.

Which brings me to my next layer of forgiveness: yourself. It is often so subtle that we blame ourselves because we find other people to blame first but soon enough, we realize that we are holding ourselves back. We eventually reach an age where we realize no one else is responsible for us. Then, we must take a serious look in the mirror to meet with ourselves about the pain we have actually caused ourselves.

We must acknowledge the messes *we* have made and start cleaning them up. This might include apologies, retractions, and peace offerings. This might include a big shift or change to the way we do things. This might mean ending relationships, jobs, or behaviors, but in any sense, it is a clean-up season.

Our custom homebuilding career was not intended to be something I did full-time for the rest of my life. It was simply a step in our journey toward creating financial freedom. When I was having those visceral reactions and knew it was time to move on to the next step in my life, I judged myself a bit for getting so busy and so far in over my head. I had to forgive myself before I could make a shift in a positive direction. I had messes to clean up and contracts to complete but once I did, I started feeling better. I had to practice forgiveness and remember one of the most important lessons of life; we are all always doing our best.

I have gotten things wrong many times when I thought I was doing my best and it is self-forgiveness that helps me bounce back from a challenging letdown. As an endless optimist, I tend to leap to solving problems and I have prematurely put myself into situations that I later realized I had acted too fast and stepped into too far. I did this dozens of times before truly learning the lessons and learning to lean back before I react.

No matter what messes you have been put into or gotten yourself into, forgiveness is a major factor in how your future looks. For starters, you have to forgive yourself for how long you feel it has taken you to learn this information. We never truly learn anything before we are ready to receive it so no matter what age or stage you are in, what you learned from this book is perfect for you right now. If you read it again in a year, you would gather new insights and awareness on the next level of your journey.

The same goes for those messy life lessons; no matter how many break-ups you've been through, no matter how many times you've gotten yourself into debt, no matter how many perceived failures you can count, you've learned something new every time. You will have to repeat it however many times necessary until you get the lesson for yourself. There's no cheating life, not really. You can't copy the kid next to you. You have to pass your own tests and you will be put through them until you do.

This is where your message is born. You solidify your lessons and awareness in the trenches of life, only to come out triumphantly teaching them to others in an attempt to spare them even one round in the ring. Based on the unique path you have walked; you have a particular understanding of life that will be helpful and important to our collective consciousness. You sharing your message on whatever scale you see fit is the difference you came to make.

For some, that looks like breaking those generational abuse patterns and raising a happy, healthy family. Others might be compelled to be leaders in their communities, schools, and churches. Some people decide to step up on larger platforms in politics or, like myself, the self-education realm. The possibilities are endless. However you choose to take a leadership role in your life, you will have a message and lessons to share.

I have successfully progressed through the messes to have arrived at a place in my life where my message is that you can have it all, you can do it too, and there's room for you. I have tested these theories and against plenty of odds have created a life I have always dreamt about. I am crystal clear on the abundance available in life and have decided to make it my job to teach people how to attract that abundance.

You have a message in you, and I invite you to consider what it is. I have a few questions to help you more clearly discover and shape that message. Before answering these questions, I invite you to drop your shoulders and loosen your jaw. These aren't really mind, logic, and strategy questions. They are questions for your heart and soul so direct your focus toward your heart as you read these and then instead of answering them, listen for what your heart has to say.

 # Higher Purpose

How has your life and story shaped who you have become?

What messes have you emerged from?

What got you out of those messes?

What did you learn from those challenges and trials?

In what ways have you triumphed over life's tribulations?

If you could give a younger version of yourself advice right now, what would it be?

What has been the most valuable lesson of your life?

What would you want to teach the next generation?

Okay, now take a few more deep breaths and drop even deeper into your heart. You may even sit still for a few moments of silence before moving on.
What is your divine role and purpose here in this lifetime?

What message did you come here to deliver?

Who did you come here to deliver that message to?

What legacy do you hope to leave?

What do you hope people remember about you?

If you feel fully into it What would you say at your own eulogy—this is one of the most powerful exercises anyone could ever take on.

You, my friend, have an important role and message that you came here to deliver. You have a presence and gifts that the world needs. You showing up fully for life will have life showing up fully for you. Step out of your silent suffering and let your mess become your message. The world is waiting to hear your story. It is time for you to speak up.

Chapter 20

There's Room for You

"You belong here just as much as any other individual and you deserve freedom and peace as much as anybody else. Most importantly, at the end of the day, it is going to be you who grants yourself permission to have it."

Whenever we start a new venture, it can seem big and intimidating. When I have dreams, I can see and sense their entire manifestation and I can become fixated on the vision as a whole. In my past, this has given me tunnel vision and I would blow past some of the smaller details and mini victories because I was aiming for the mountain top. This approach is what leads to burnout and frustration, but I want to teach others that the journey is just as important as the destination.

One of the rings I wear every day was the ring I bought when my wedding ring didn't fit during both of my pregnancies. It wasn't until my second pregnancy that I noticed that there was a message engraved on the inside of it that read *life is about the journey, not the destination.* I still continue to wear that ring every day as a reminder to enjoy the journey.

Whenever I slow down enough to realize where we are in life, I have always found myself astonished. This didn't always happen because I was super present. It often occurred because someone else was amazed at Noah's and my achievements.

In some of our real estate courses, we would be sitting in rooms with already high-achieving millionaires and others who worked with or were related to billionaires who lived these seemingly lavish lives. We would listen to the connections these people had and the companies they worked for, and I would have to consciously not let my face tell on me. I had to keep my jaw from dropping open or visibly revealing my starstruck feeling when they would talk about their yachts, mansions, and inner circle associates. *How are we in this class with these people?* I would wonder.

Noah and I would sit timidly in these rooms until it was our turn to introduce ourselves. I would share about our current projects, businesses, and investments. Noah usually kept quiet and had me do the talking first and he usually opened up more as the classes went on.

To my surprise, it was *their* jaws that would drop. These remarkably successful people would clamor over the company and legacy we built. They were amazed at how we could do so much in so little time in such a little town and how well it was working for us.

This was a very interesting and out-of-body experience for us. No matter how much we achieved in our careers, we have always still felt like ourselves; two ambitious 'farm kids' from Southern Wisconsin. At our core, we've stayed the same Becky and Noah that started out on their journey to financial freedom. I like to joke because by comparison to our financially independent peers, especially in those real estate environments, we don't show *our* wealth. No matter how much we make, Noah will always be the one wearing a camouflage hunting hat, cut-off shirt, jeans, and boots staying quiet in the corner of the room during an event from which he later leaves in his loud, diesel, one ton pick-up truck. I've joked about how we look like two hillbillies from the Midwest amongst the elite at some of these conferences. There have been times where we unintentionally showed up to black tie events in jeans and boots, ruining the black-tie affair. However, we have won some of the most prestigious awards and honors amongst those groups and we have stood on those stages as equals.

Just because we would rather sport Carhartt gear more often than heels and ties didn't mean we couldn't do business equal or better than anyone else, but we had to adjust the way we viewed our business and partnership. We have achieved some incredible feats in our short career in real estate as first-generation entrepreneurs. We have been considered as big dogs on the playing field by comparison. I had gotten such tunnel vision for the dream that I didn't exactly realize we had achieved most of it.

At most of these real estate courses, people would come up to us and ask us how we did what we did. Again, this amazed me. How were we further along than these people who seemed so well off? Well, my friend, there is a valuable lesson that I want to teach you about who you are and how gifted you are.

We all have these sets of gifts, insights, and perspectives that distinguish us from the crowd. We all have natural talents and personal forms of reasoning that when put to use, put us a head above the rest. We are often known for these gifts, but do not know it ourselves because the trick is, our talent precedes us. So often, we overlook or even downplay our talents and gifts because they come as second nature to us. We assume everyone can do that talent as easily as we can and so we devalue it as our gift.

One thing that happened in our career is that we were so focused on financial freedom that whenever we sold a new house, we put that income straight into the bank and never really related to it as income. We may have doubled our profit at any given time and didn't realize it because we were laser-focused on the final outcome. Well, we were doubling our profit and our equity and our property and our experience and our empire. Month by month and year by year, we were becoming one of the most prominent businesses around. I got sort of bug-eyed the day I really understood exactly how far we had come and where we stood in the crowd.

I also had to accept that we knew our stuff. Maybe we weren't just two humble farmers from Nowheresville. Maybe we were the Hurleys of Hurley Ranch and maybe we did in fact know what the heck we were doing.

I finally solidified this lesson for myself when I began re-branding and upleveling the real estate investing branch of our company. Sure, I had learned a thing or two in real estate and homebuilding and of course we were rockin' right along, but when I branched out into the more sophisticated version of the real estate investing world, I figured we needed some help. I assumed that because we were new to this level of investing, we didn't have everything we needed to make our brand a success, so I hired people to help us roll out the plan and build the brand. I assumed I needed to hire next-level people if I wanted to go to the next level.

When I explained what we wanted and needed, I was offered a roughly $200,000 contract to launch a year-long plan that would surely take us where we were headed. My lender was shaking in his boots that I would agree to spend that much money on marketing but I felt safe investing in the future of the new direction we were heading. I said yes, began making plans with the company and to kick off the contract, and we headed out to Colorado to meet with the executive team and sign paperwork.

Noah and I made a whole trip of that meeting. We road tripped without the kids, just like our very first drive to Florida. In true Becky fashion, I even brought some books to read out loud. We stopped at some new spots and treated ourselves to a great time together. It was fabulous.

What didn't turn out so fabulous was how we felt in that meeting about the plan being put in place. When we got there and the team was briefing us on what they would do and our part in it, something didn't sit right. They were telling me what I had already known, just in fancier lingo. I realized that what they were bringing to the table wasn't really what I needed. I had grown another business using many of the same tactics and approaches that I would be doing anyway and knew exactly what to do. I found myself in another situation in which I tried to prevent my jaw from dropping open in front of everybody.

I knew I didn't want to make this investment. I have no fear about investments, but this one didn't feel aligned for me, and I knew I was going to have to break the contract. We left that meeting and I shared my feelings with Noah, and he agreed. We didn't sleep much that night due to the aches in our stomach from these realizations. He trusted my judgment going into the meeting and he trusted it coming out. That's what I love about that man, but I will swoon over him at another time. The lesson was that we stayed on the same page and knew we could launch our new dream as successfully as we had achieved every other one.

The next morning, I let the team know that we would be canceling the contract and I was handed a $15,000 cancellation fee, which sort of took my breath away. At the same time, I related to that $15,000 as a statement to myself that *yes, I know my stuff* and I am going to finally own it. We are two insanely successful, heart-centered people and we are going to teach people how to reach financial freedom from a heart-centered place. I have built an empire from the ground up and I could do it a hundred times over. Except now, I will lead others to build their own empires.

I feel called to share this because something happens to people in their lives which causes them to finally accept, acknowledge, and value their gifts. I am sad to say that this doesn't happen for everyone but anyone who is successful in their field has had to cross this bridge. You have to reach a point when you value your talents enough to get paid for them instead of paying others or losing money getting used for your talents insufficiently.

In this example, it took a trip to Colorado to realize our gifts. I made the assumption that because that team was located somewhere else, they had superior skills, insights, and leverage than we did. I had to cross a few states and get a look for myself to realize that wasn't true. You have to sort of 'get out of your bubble' to observe others' work or achievements to comprehend where you stand in the crowd. We would bury our heads in work and hardly ever come out to find out how we were doing amongst the industry standards. We thought we had to go outside of ourselves to find the answers when we had been doing the work well all along. The way to success is not by having other people do it for you, it is by getting up and trying. It is when you explore outside of your comfort zone that you find out your work is comparable or maybe even superior. I have proven this to myself time and time again but now I *know* it in my bones.

You will have to take a look for yourself, too. Your writing may be better than you think, but you might never know if you don't share it. Your voice may shock people, but you'd never know unless you sing. Your art, management skills, cooking, or building may never reach its full potential because you won't expose it to the world and further develop it. Well, I want you to know that there is room for you, too.

There are so many talented people who underestimate their gifts and never end up recognized for them. More specifically, there are talented people who are not talented businesspeople or marketers. Therefore, they don't know how to make a living with their skills. I also want to be clear that you do not have to use your gifts by starting your own business. There are tons of jobs and careers with other companies that will highlight your gifts and pay you to be operating in your area of expertise, but you must become willing to put yourself out there.

I want to address a myth that discourages so many talented folks from putting themselves out there: *the market is saturated with people like me.* For starters, no one can duplicate the way you do what you specifically do. If we believed the market was saturated when we started Hurley Ranch, we would have never been able to do what we did in the industry. That is not an attitude that will get you to the top of your field. If you say there are already too many computer programmers, artists, singers, or carpenters, then you will have eliminated yourself from the running because those who are being seen and hired are those who believe there is room for them in the industry.

Another myth that I want to debunk is that money, success, or abundance of any kind is a 'zero sum game.' The concept of a zero-sum game is that there is a finite number of resources and that another person's gain is another person's loss. That fits into the pie idea that there is a certain amount available, and that we must learn how to split it fairly or you must figure out how to get a bigger portion. Historically, this has caused competition over collaboration in our society. In order to make the money or reach the heights you dream of, you are going to need to make an internal adjustment to this belief.

There is enough money, success, abundance, and resources to go around. Any shortages are perception because abundance and lack are mindsets, not concrete realities. Now, again, before you slam this book down and never return, consider a few things. I completely understand when times get challenging, funds get low, and things are falling apart. I understand how challenging it can be to get out of a hole, get the medical attention you need, or get the basics of food, shelter, and water. I know that if you had more control, you wouldn't be in those situations, and I am here to help you alter that.

One important thing to consider is that times are not *always* tough. Meaning, there are countless examples, even in your own life, of the natural ebbs and flows. There are plenty of examples of brighter days. There are tough seasons and there are winning seasons. There are sowing seasons and there are harvesting seasons. An important part of this lesson is becoming more intentional about the dips and peaks and not panicking or quitting when times get tough. You must learn to recognize the turning of the tables, knowing that dark seasons don't last forever. This will help you shift out of the zero-sum mindset. Money, resources, and abundance are always in circulation. It never remains stagnant; therefore, you can always acquire more.

There is enough to go around. There is enough for you. There is room for you at the table of success. There is room for you at the bank, at the restaurant, and in the hotel, school, or church. There is room for you on the stage or in the office. There is room for you in this world. You belong here just as much as any other individual and you deserve freedom and peace as much as anybody else. Most importantly, at the end of the day, it is going to be you who grants yourself permission to have it.

You will have to learn to value yourself, your gifts, your craft, your knowledge, and your skills to take the time to develop and offer them in a way that helps you make a living. I understand it feels competitive out there but that is because so much of the population is still playing a zero-sum game where one doesn't exist. Don't buy into the illusion. People who have a wealth mindset don't play by following what society tells them to do, they play by a belief system that they can have it all. Because they are willing to believe it, they are able to have it. You will have to shift your focus from getting your piece of the pie to receiving everything you know you deserve and more.

It can be hard to believe that when it feels like you are running into barrier after barrier. So, let's demystify another myth. Failure is the end of your dreams. Y'all, I have already addressed the mountains of mistakes or messes I have piled up in my life and I stand on top of it shouting, *"You can have it all!"* If you spend all your time sad about what didn't work, you will miss out on the opportunity of understanding why.

So often when we are chasing a dream, we are really developing a fuller vision that we couldn't see from our previous level of comprehension. This means that as time goes on, the full picture unfolds to reveal new bits and pieces of all that is possible in our lives. We must remain open when situations or relationships don't pan out as we originally planned.

Keep in mind as you decide to show up for your dream that when one door seems to be slammed in your face, that another one will open. A more advanced perspective of this idea is that it is not always doors of opportunity that open right away, rather, doors of awareness. When I felt like the teaching door was closed on me, it forced me to look elsewhere in my heart for what I was passionate about and how I could apply that passion in my career. That led to my non-profit work and further developed me as a businesswoman. When the non-profit door closed, it yet again forced me to apply new passion and newly-developed skills to my entrepreneurship and the rest is history.

What there is to know when you feel like room isn't being made for you where you expect it, is very likely because you are being redirected to consider something new or an alternative application of your talent. If you spend less time wallowing about how it didn't go, you can more quickly find out how it is destined to go and you can make your way to personal and financial freedom in a much more fluid manner.

One thing I have learned over the years of trial and error is that anything inauthentic falls apart. When we chase a dream that we conjured up in our mind's eye, it may come together by force, but it will unravel very naturally because it is not a part of the greater plan. The laws of nature always win on this because you have a very important role in your time on the planet. We come to serve in our greatest capacity and anything you build to uphold your comfort zone will become hard work to maintain as it ever-so-predictably crumbles from underneath you.

I don't mean to sound scary or threatening when I say that, but I do hope to spare you a lot of trouble and heartache by encouraging you to follow what is in your heart, instead of your head. If you are trying to build anything from ego, it will likely cause you a lot of turmoil until you dismantle it for a truer and aligned life.

I share all of this in hopes of saving you some time and energy. I urge you to follow your heart and passion. I want to make it abundantly clear that there is room for your gifts. That is why you were born with them. You came here with these skills to make your contribution to humanity. You will be most empowered to do that if you honor your God-given talents.

It's okay if it feels scary but if you have learned anything from me at this point, I hope you have gathered that the risk is worth the reward. Also, that it is safer to take risks than you may have originally thought. I am clear that when we surrender to our callings and follow the path of our passion, a way will be made. A seat will be prepared. Resources will manifest. Practice faith and trust and you can trust that room will be reserved, just for you, in all your splendor and glory.

Chapter 21

You Can Have It All

"Even if your current situation is completely different from what you desire, the next step toward your goals is to hold your focus."

We are arriving at the top of the mountain for our time together. We have been through the trenches, climbed walls, overcome obstacles, and we are getting to higher altitudes with a more expansive view. We have cleared and released a lot of obstacles and gotten clearer on who you are and what you want. Now, let's really integrate that new belief system deep into your being.

Repeat after me:

I can have it all.

Immediately check in, did you believe yourself?

Repeat it five more times:

I can have it all.

I *can* have it all.

I *can have* it all.

I *can have it all.*

I CAN HAVE IT ALL!

Good, now take a deep inhale and exhale a big sigh of relief as you acknowledge your new belief system. No doubt it will take some more integrating, but we are off to a great start. My personal belief that anything is possible was always there, but it still took me a few tries to really reach levels of abundance that could manifest my vision into full form.

For example, during my work with the non-profit, I was at the top of my game. I was excelling within my role, making a difference in the organization, and having a great time along the way. I was making friends, having a blast networking with farm families, and really loving my job. I 'had it all' by my definition at the time.

Naturally, it got to a point where I was ready for the next level. After a few years in an entry level position at the non-profit, I could sense I was ready to take it to the next level. Although I was doing well in my current position, I had a strong urge to level up, but I didn't quite know what that looked like.

Very soon after I started feeling this way, the top-ranking position in our organization opened up. That opening was three levels above my current standing with the company, but you can bet that Rule Breaker Becky put in her application. Skipping all the middle levels of the organization and heading straight to the top was a long shot, but I applied anyway. I knew I had nothing to lose and to be totally honest, that was the only position I was really interested in if I was going to stay with the organization.

Staying entry level was not what I wanted for my life. I wasn't seeking comfort; I was seeking growth and new opportunities. I did get an interview, but it may have been out of obligation and comedic relief for the interview committee because I did not get the job. I didn't feel disappointed, however, it was an awakening experience.

As I mentioned in the last chapter, when a door closes in life, it opens up a new awareness in your being. Applying for the top spot was my acknowledgment to myself that I was ready for more. It didn't matter that they didn't give it to me, I just realized that if I were to continue in this non-profit position, I would become stagnant, and that was the last thing I wanted. I knew it deep down, but I hadn't really learned to pay attention to those visceral reactions just yet. I kept that job another month before I could no longer ignore how I felt.

I drove home from one of my last meetings in tears. I'm talking about mascara-streaks-all down-my-face-and-neck crying; that sobbing that comes from the depth of your tired soul.

I wasn't upset because the meeting went bad or anything wrong had happened. I just *knew* and accepted right then and there that I wasn't growing in that position anymore, nor would I. It was time to be done with that organization. The next week, I told my boss that I would be leaving the organization. He understood and didn't challenge me. He knew I was made for more, too. Even though I loved my job, it was time to walk away and make room for my career as an entrepreneur who had no cap on her potential or position.

I have nuggets of advice in this chapter that have helped me reach unbelievable heights in my lifetime that I know will support you in 'having it all' for yourself as well.

The number one rule of *having* it all is clarifying what *it all* is. Early on, in chapter 6, I asked you to become willing to dream big, and then bigger. I asked you to get really clear on the life you want and what having it all means, so you should have a good foundation for this chapter. If you didn't create clarity in chapter 6, I encourage you to revisit that work to empower the progress we are making in this part of the book.

In that chapter I asked you to write down exactly what you want. At this moment, I want you to consider your age. Twenty-year-old Becky did not want all the same things as thirty-year-old Becky. Having it all looked different at twenty-five than thirty-five. It will look different at forty, fifty, sixty, and so on. Therefore, you will have to revisit what having it all means at the different stages of your life.

In fact, having it all may even be different now than when you read chapter 6. The power play in manifestation and having it all is checking in on your definition of 'it all' frequently. This will help you adjust over time. You can stop chasing goals that are no longer in alignment with where you are headed in life. It will make it easier to course correct when you have reached a certain milestone or no longer have the same goals. You may outgrow certain desires. The destination you once valued may become irrelevant once you have had more exposure to it. These are all very valuable considerations when creating your dream life.

Sometimes, we want things just out of habit or conditioning because we have always wanted them. If we really take a serious look, our grown selves may not need or want the goals a younger version of ourselves set, but we may have become so used to wanting that goal that we chase after it by default. I wanted to inherit our family farm so badly until I realized it was not worth the turmoil it caused in my life. I discovered that I could create my own life on my own farm with my own family and when I made that course correction, my life took a turn for the better. My health and happiness increased tenfold when I released an outdated desire. I encourage you to really evaluate what you say you want, especially if you have been saying you want it for a long time.

This may require simplifying or expanding your dreams about your life. I mentioned how getting to any mountain top simply reveals new peaks to set your sights on. Becoming more intentional about choosing a life that fulfills you, instead of just getting excited about the chase, can add a decade to your lifetime. Chasing is tiresome and lackluster. The thrill of the catch lasts about as long as a fish out of water. Hint: not long.

This brings me to a really important point about the chase and becoming a more mindful manifester—jealousy. It is very natural that when you see someone else living the life you want to live, having the things you want to have, and enjoying the things that you want to enjoy, you might find yourself jealous of that person. You may even find yourself dangerously envious of that person. This may cause you to look down on yourself or wish badly upon them. Since I trust that is not your intention, let's address this issue.

When you get a jealous urge or judgment of another, it is important to become observant of yourself. If you find yourself thinking *it must be nice* or some other envious thought, that is a communication from within that you have a desire for what they have and they are activating the awareness that *your* desire has yet to manifest. You are feeling the missing of that thing in your life.

That simply means that you know what you want, and someone is showing you that what you want is possible. The feeling of jealousy is that you are feeling challenged to achieve that goal when you might not feel like you can. Jealousy is very much an illusion because you are comparing your day one to someone's day one thousand. The sting of jealousy is being present to the gap between you and what you want. This is not useful because it will keep you trapped in judgment instead of aligned action. This will murder your enthusiasm, willingness, and possibility for achieving your goals. So instead of staying jealous, accept the challenge and get up to the aligned actions that would help you manifest that goal!

To the point of getting clear about having it all, it would serve you greatly to make a vision board of the life you are trying to manifest. A vision board is a collage of pictures of your dreams. This can be as concrete or abstract as you like. For example, say you want to travel to Hawaii. Print out a picture of a place you'd like to see in Hawaii, like a beach, a restaurant, or a waterfall, and put that on your vision board. I manifested my big, beautiful gray GMC Yukon this way, even when I could hardly afford a small car at the time. This can be more abstract and represent the vibe of the life you want. This may include colors, words, and images that activate a feeling in you; the feeling you want to be having in your dream life. You know, like when you are financially free.

Instead of staring at someone else's life with judgment, create a board that represents your future life and start to train your mind to see it all as possible and available. The more you see it, the more you will believe it. The more you believe it, the more you will achieve it because you will attract it. You will become a magnet for the life you put up on your vision board.

Another nugget I would like to teach you, and maybe reassure you with is not to worry about 'the how' of the process. Your dream life will manifest naturally if you follow the instructions in this book. I mentioned how all the co-creative components will synchronize and come together when you set your intentions to have a certain life experience. This concept is known as the Law of Attraction. Explained very briefly, 'what you think about you bring about.' All the components will work themselves out.

Even if your current situation is completely different from what you desire, the next step toward your goals is to hold your focus. Each morning, close your eyes and focus on the life you want the most. Think about how awesome it would be to have it. This is the application of your new visualization skills here.

When I do this, I get fully into it. It often brings me to tears because of how real my dreams can seem. I think about my dreams and how great it will be to be living them. When I think about how amazing it will feel once that dream is realized, I cry tears of gratitude over it. I cry tears about how many times this practice has worked for me. I cry about the current reality I am living that was once a dream board.

There is a way to bring the dreams on your vision board closer right here, right now. Having the dreams that have only existed in your mind and heart manifest into your physical reality is such an emotional experience. Practice bringing your dreams to life right now, feel into the *feeling* of having what you want. You don't have to wait till you have it. If it stirs up a positive buzz of excitement within you, then you know you have a dream that you truly desire. Those are gold. Hold the vision and take the aligned steps toward their manifestation.

Yes, you *do* have steps to take. You have an important role in the realization of your dreams. If you can feel into your dream life with visualization, it is very likely that you will get a hint of inspiration about what to do next. You will be able to tell what your next steps are and it becomes your job to follow through on them. You can start taking those steps, even baby steps, toward making this dream a reality.

Follow-through is the key to success when it comes to co-creating with the Universe. The Universe rewards action takers. Even if it is scary or you feel unsure, putting yourself out there and heading in the direction of your dreams will pay off later. It won't be too much later if you get started right now.

You *can* have it all, my dear friend. You have made your way through a book designed to help you navigate building your dreams. I have shared so much of my heart and journey because it has naturally paved a way for you to follow with fewer obstacles. If I can help you have your dream life even a minute quicker than it took me, I will be so satisfied.

The world is transforming, and progress is happening at lightning speed these days. To keep up with the pace, clearing your body, heart, and mind of any dead weight will help you float toward your dreams a lot more easily. I want to encourage you to keep creating clarity because the last nugget I want to offer you in this chapter is that vague goals lead to vague results. If you refuse to get clear and make clear requests, you will haphazardly be manifesting a life that is only some of what you are hoping for.

You absolutely can have it all, as long as you know what that means for you.

Chapter 22

Your Turn

"You start with yourself, but your ripple effect
will no doubt create massive waves everywhere."

We made it! No, I won't act like I've been here before. I just wrote my first book! The first book of many, mind you. In the process of putting this masterpiece together, I was able to pull apart all the important components of the many books I want to write. The theme of this one became personal and financial freedom through healing, but there will be more about financial strategy, real estate, parenting, business ownership, and more. I love that we have made it to this point together and I look forward to supporting you along your journey in the future. If we aren't already connected, let's be friends on social media @msbeckyhurley and be sure to check out my website at www.beckyhurley.com.

We have arrived at the point where you take on your life with the clarity and guidance you came to this book for. I formally pass the torch over to you as you head down your path of success.

When I first started out on my journey of transformation, something that made me nervous about the end of books or courses was maintaining the momentum I created within the pages or program. I was afraid that my feeling of high vibration would plummet once I stopped reading, listening, learning, and attending. Over time, I learned how to integrate the work long after a life-changing course to create a more lasting impact.

There are two major factors I would like to teach you as you apply all this new information into your life. One, you *will* get triggered or off track again. Two, you will sometimes feel like you are up against a wall you have already surpassed.

When you think you have healed all there is to heal within you, you start to feel good. You have a better sense of self, you are making positive changes, and manifesting better results in your life. This is a wonderful experience, and we can get pretty attached to this good feeling.

Then, your Uncle Bob makes some backhanded comment at Christmas, and you are flung right back into your childhood wounding. You start spiraling, questioning everything, doubting any and all progress, and start cursing your foolish attempt at believing things could ever get better. Sound familiar? Yeah, I get it. Good news, this is a predictable part of the work.

Because you are a human, you will never be fully enlightened, zenned out, and completely blissful one hundred percent of the time. It is your expectation to be totally healed that will trigger a meltdown. Being a human on Earth has its challenges, predictable and unpredictable. You must come to accept that you will get triggered, disempowered, frustrated, annoyed, challenged, and more. There will be days you want to quit and days that you feel like you have forgotten everything you learned. I want to assure you that isn't true.

When you get activated and start slipping down the slope of misery, simply *notice* that it is happening. You don't have to change or fix it. You don't have to halt your negative emotions. You don't have to become instantly happy, rather, you get to feel those negative feelings.

Toxic positivity says *good vibes only,* but the reality is you will face some tough situations and tougher people. This is no reason to throw your arms up and consider yourself a lost cause. In fact, it is the opposite. This is an opportunity to apply your new practices and awarenesses. You have the right to your reactions in the face of a trigger and you must consider them messengers of what remains unhealed within you. Being mindful is a lifelong journey so please don't be too hard on yourself. You will have the chance to investigate why that memory, person, or situation upset you and take on the next layer of healing, blessing, and releasing that pain.

This will get you right back on track with your transformation which can then run you right into point number two. You will experience an evolved version of an old wound when you continuously uplevel. You are not repeating an old lesson, you are passing a higher level of that same lesson. You will know the difference between repeating or passing based on the quality of your life.

For example, I am prone to burnout. I did it in teaching and homebuilding, I've done it in parenting, and I have caught myself doing it in my brand building. It is a habit that has evolved with me. Whenever I catch myself in a burnout cycle, I first catch it and then feel my feelings about it. Then, I am clear enough to evaluate the situation. I ran my burnout cycle a few times in homebuilding and that was me repeating the lesson. With each uplevel in my career, I was passing the next step of deconditioning that habit. I would look around my life and take note about how I was doing significantly better than the last time this habit took over subconsciously. I would also notice how it was happening less frequently and I would notice it much sooner. This. Is. Progress.

We must stay conscious of our areas of challenge because they are our personal areas of growth, and I would bet a lot of money that they are also your areas of expertise. I teach about burnout in this book because I have learned so much about it in my transformation. I have mastered recognizing and overcoming it in a way that it no longer runs my life. The old Becky identities that needed to prove herself, win, compete, and achieve no longer run my life. Those versions of me still like to show up from time to time, but I kindly let them know they do not have a say in how my life will go from here on out.

You have this same power. You will continue to grow and be challenged by that growth, but at no point have you fallen backwards, lost momentum, or forgotten what you've learned. You cannot forget. It is imprinted in you and is now operating in your subconscious. You are in this transformation situation for the long haul, baby! So, now it is time to accept it and your role in the forward progress of the world. You start with yourself, but your ripple effect will no doubt create massive waves everywhere.

So, to you I say, *get out there!* Go make a positive difference in this world! You have all the tools you need to heal your heart and transform your life. You have all the knowledge within you to chase your dreams head on. You have done the work of creating your personal freedom that unchains you to create your financial freedom with ease and flow. I am so grateful to have spent this time with you, but now it is your turn to step out boldly and share your innate gifts and insights.

Tell your story.
Own your skills.
Share your unique perspective.
Hold your vision.
Trust the process.
Unleash your heart.
Build your dreams.

Acknowledgments

I knew I would write this book for over a decade. Five years before, I journaled that I would write a book. To fulfill that declaration brings me such joy and satisfaction. I'm so proud and honored to bring this book to you. This is my gift to the world, tied up with a bow, presented with honor and delicacy.

I cannot think of a better way to honor my ancestors, guardian angels, and God than to share this message. This message is one my soul has meant for me to share. My purpose on Earth guided me to get these words on these pages. I hope that this message will delight, inform, inspire and transform you.

Even though it's been on my heart and soul to write these pages, this book is made possible by the amazing team surrounding and supporting me:

My husband, Noah, my love, my light, my foundation, and my rock. You are everything to me and I love you so much.

My children, Tesla and Jace. My precious gifts, my blessing, it is an honor to be your mother. I'm so proud of you and I love you. I am a better person because of you.

My supportive team of coaches and friends. Abigail Gazda, you are such a gift from God. I have chills writing this from how God brought you into my life to help bring this book to life. Words cannot describe my love and appreciation for all you have done. Thank you.

My healing team, coaching group and friends. You know who you are. The ones I have cried with, prayed with and laughed with through this whole journey. Thank you for your wise words, your beautiful spirit, and your love and encouragement. I have grown and healed so much with your guiding light. Thank you.

To all of you reading this, loved ones, friends, colleagues, clients, and readers from near and far, I love and appreciate you so much. Everyone who has had a part in my life has had a part in this book. Thank you.

Author Bio

Farm girl turned multi-million-dollar business mogul, Becky Hurley, is living proof that you can go through hard times and come out the other side. With a feminine flair to her gritty upbringing, she has set out to share a message of inspiration with the world.

With a passion for dreaming big and bringing dreams to life, she loves to shine the light of hope for those looking to build their future of personal and financial freedom. Having faced years of trauma in her childhood, Becky teaches her readers that you can go through abusive situations and go on to create a happy, healthy, prosperous life. She does this as a speaker, podcaster, blogger and energetic being by sharing many how-to's of healing to reach ultimate levels of success and happiness.

Becky has been known to build dreams as well as subdivisions, commercial and residential rental complexes, and luxury, custom homes with her husband Noah, as the co-founders of a real estate investing, development, and general contracting company. With an edge in real estate investing, Becky teaches her community how to make smart power moves while maintaining wellbeing and fun.

From farm girl to teacher, to homebuilder, to real estate investor, to self-help educator, Becky shares her message through books, speaking engagements, podcasts and more. She also enjoys homesteading, farming, reading books, and chasing her own next dream. You can connect with and learn from her at hello@buildingdreams.co.

Becky resides on her farm in Wisconsin with her husband, Noah, and two children, Tesla and Jace.

www.ingramcontent.com/pod-product-compliance
Lightning Source LLC
Chambersburg PA
CBHW050446150626
46551CB00029B/1790